AN INCREDIBLE GOD

China and Her Encounter with God

Werner Bürklin

AN INCREDIBLE GOD
CHINA AND HER ENCOUNTER WITH GOD

iUniverse books may be ordered through booksellers or by contacting:

iUniverse
1663 Liberty Drive
Bloomington, IN 47403
www.iuniverse.com
1-800-Authors (1-800-288-4677)

ISBN: 978-1-4917-7555-4 (sc)
ISBN: 978-1-4917-7554-7 (e)

Library of Congress Control Number: 2015916933

Print information available on the last page.

iUniverse rev. date: 10/07/2015

Contents

PREFACE

Rickshaw-coolies no longer run in the streets of Shanghai, nor in any city of China. Years ago, rickshaws were widely used to comfortably transport people. They were first introduced in Japan in the late 19ᵗʰ Century and then spread into many Asian countries, including China. The coolies—also called runners—were proud of their rickshaws and kept them clean and tidy. Some of the runners beefed them up with fancy paraphernalia, such as shiny lamps on the sides or extravagant covers. The real swanky sprinter, often employed by wealthy merchants, even wore white gloves, and that proudly.

I personally miss those coolies; for me they were so strong and resilient. Not an extra pound of fat on their bodies and always ready to serve! Others saw it differently: "Rickshaws became an embarrassment to modernizing urban elites of the Third World," Chris Carlsson states in his book *Critical Mass: Bicycling's Defiant Celebration*, "and were widely banned, in part because they were symbolic, not of modernity, but of a feudal world of openly marked class distinctions." As to me, though, I admire those sturdy coolies for their willingness to work hard. Most of them broke out from poverty-stricken rural areas and proved to the world, that such able bodied men can make a worthwhile and decent living.

By the 1950s rickshaws slowly disappeared, and pedicaps (German-made cycle rickshaws) were used instead. Those were much more efficient and, of course, faster.

It is believed that runners often covered twenty to thirty miles in a day at an average speed of five miles per hour. Those were hard-working men! I was always fascinated by them, even though I sometimes played pranks—not to say, mischiefs—on them. Showing off to my friends, I would call a rickshaw over. The runner would lower the vehicle so that I could step in, but, as he was turning around to pull up the handles, I would step off. Suddenly without the expected weight behind him, the poor coolie was being inadvertently thrown off balance and would stumble to regain his equilibrium. We all laughed hysterically. Shame on us!

Coolies, during my time, were still being exploited by the gentry. They lived a tough life and were extremely poor. But they were a major force in the developing country. Now they are gone.

Let us now look at a different aspect that made parts of China what it was recently: a lost generation (see also the chapter in this book on China's fourth generation).

The term "lost generation" refers to the people, who, during the Cultural Revolution (1966-76), were forced to miss out on educational privileges that others in other countries enjoyed. With the absurd and irrational policies, which Mao had thrust on China's population, an entire generation suffered immensely. As a consequence, China spiraled downward with accelerating speed, from which she recovered later on only after a super effort by Deng Xiaoping. The people caught up in this generation became desperate.

What could and should, and what actually was done about it? We shall get back to it later in the book.

But one more thing I must mention. I wrote this book to expose certain aspects of how different nations live. Ancient Asia was very dissimilar from ancient Europe, and todays Europe is somewhat different from the United States. But there are also similarities. However, cultural differences do remain and are apparent.

Therefore, I will include a chapter on one of America's President.

So far, the United States has had forty-four presidents—some were good, some outstanding, and others mediocre or incompetent. One remarkable man in my mind was George W. Bush. Not everyone will agree with me, which is normal, but everybody can agree about his solid Christian beliefs, his impeccable personal life, and his integrity. I will compare him with some of the leaders in China. I will not do this in an explicit way, but will write about him in such a way, that you will understand what I mean. One whole chapter is allocated to him.

All in all, most importantly God is the focus of this book. Wherever we go, whether in China or in any other country, we find the handiwork of God. He is all-powerful, loving and caring, truly an incredible God.

CHAPTER 1

Understanding China

C hina is a country with a rich, recorded history of over, some say, six-thousand years. The Chinese people are generally a very proud and patriotic people. You will also find them mostly cordial and kind. Especially the Chinese Christians are very warm and compassionate. You will notice that no matter where you go, they will always warmly welcome and accommodate you.

The Chinese language has many different dialects, though the written language is the same throughout China. The pronunciation of the characters varies widely in different regions. In order to facilitate better communication among the Chinese, Mandarin was chosen as the standard spoken language. This happened soon after the last monarchy government, Qing Dynasty (1644-1911), had been overturned.

When Mao Zedong (also known as Mao Tse-tung; notice that all Chinese names of people are expressed in the "Chinese way," i.e., surname/last name allocated first, followed by the person's given/first name) founded the current People's Republic of China in 1949, Mandarin (or *putonghua* or *guoyü* in Chinese) continued as the official spoken language. Mandarin is now taught in schools throughout China, including Hong Kong—where most still speak Cantonese—plus Macau and Taiwan.

Our son Erik has worked in China for many years and is therefore very knowledgeable about this country. He made several observations that I would like to share.

One of the greatest features about China is, of course, its restaurants. Chinese love to eat. This becomes a big event when people get together for dinner or lunch. They will usually sit at a round table with a lazy Susan in the center and many dishes are served. One should remember to take time when eating. You will notice the Chinese will grab a few bites here and there, and then lay down their chopsticks to break for conversation. After they have talked a few minutes, they will pick them up and continue eating. This sometimes continues for up to two hours. During a visit to China, you may be invited to one or more of these "banquets." The Chinese hosts will have a tendency to serve a little of each dish to the guests. Receive the food graciously; never say, "No." It's always a good idea to try it and if you don't like it, you can leave it. Another typical Chinese custom is to give a toast. The host usually does this; many times, it is appropriate for the guests to reciprocate.

On another subject he feels that the political situation is still somewhat volatile, and I agree. The People's Republic of China is a communist state. Communist ideology is still in the foreground among its government leaders. However, the average Chinese does not consider him/herself a communist any longer. Economic advances have improved the living conditions throughout China, and even the communist kingpins are enjoying the benefits of capitalism. When you go to major Chinese cities, you will notice modern hotels, luxury cars, beautiful, single-family homes, and all kinds of electrical devices that range from brand new DVD/VCD players to new Pentium computers and cell phones.

Criminals are dealt with swiftly. One of the safest places to live in today is China. Despite the fact that the leaders believe in communist ideology, China is experiencing tremendous freedom and with it exorbitant wealth. From a quick Google search you will find that

China in 2013 had 1.05 million millionaires (in terms of U.S. dollars), and 168 billionaires. China's GDP per capita of US$6.188 for the year 2012 is astounding compared to other third world's countries. However, 128 million people still live under the internationally accepted definition of poverty.

Since the founding of the People's Republic of China, the government has experienced numerous political and leadership changes. We are now experiencing the fifth generation: Mao Zedong, the extreme revolutionary; Deng Xiaoping, the pragmatist—he had worked in France for a short while in his late teens; Jiang Zemin, a former engineer—he had climbed the ranks in politics starting as the mayor of Shanghai; Hu Jintao, the modernist—a slick looking man in western designer clothes, and since March 2013, Xi Jinping as the new president of China.

Mao wanted to destroy the old culture. The Cultural Revolution was the darkest period of his reign. Most Chinese look back to this period with great horror. Deng began to build bridges to the West. Jiang carried out the dreams of Deng—his motto was stability. Hu led China into the 21st Century, and now Xi, somewhat a hard-liner, is guiding the nation well.

Mao attempted to destroy religion. Deng reversed that policy. Jiang tried to dovetail socialism with religious thought, Hu continued that policy and Xi followed suit.

Now let us look at the Chinese Church.

Official statistics put the number of Protestant Christians in China at approximately 20 million; this figure is clarified with the statement, "We know there are many more." However, after an intensive survey done by China Partner in all twenty-three provinces, except Tibet, plus four municipalities, five autonomous regions and two special administrative regions (Hong Kong, Macau), it is now believed that there are 38 – 40 million Protestant Christians living in China today. These include Christians in registered and unregistered churches— the so-called house churches. This was corroborated by a survey done by the East China Normal University of Shanghai, which surveyed 4,500 people. China Partner surveyed far more—7,400 people. The reason for the seeming and somewhat discrepancy in the total number of Christians in China is, that many churches have still not chosen to register with the local authorities and, therefore, accurate numbers are not available. So we have to go by surveys.

Following the Cultural Revolution, the first church to reopen was in 1979 in Ningbo, Zhejiang province, one of the oldest cities in China, dating back to 4,800 BC. After that, the reopening of old church buildings and the construction of new churches both picked up speed. As of 2013, there are over 55,000 churches and meeting places.

China has some twenty-three Bible schools and/or seminaries, with 1,800 students currently attending these theological schools. They can be categorized into three levels: national, regional, and provincial schools. Over 5,000 students have graduated since the early 80s, who have either entered into local domestic ministries or have gone on for further studies, quite a few of them, overseas. Teaching is being done by about 250 instructors of which 61 percent are graduates of the past twenty years. In addition, there are many more local training centers found in every province training lay pastors.

Statistics a few years ago, indicate there are approximately 500,000 baptisms in China each year. One of the ways the Church evangelizes its people is through weddings and funerals. Each church also sponsors its own spiritual renewal conferences. We have been told the most important way the Chinese evangelize is through personal witness and a changed life. In other words, lifestyle evangelism has been very effective in China.

In addition, there are thousands of home/family fellowship groups (*jiating jiaohui*, or, literally, house churches), most of which are located in the country side but can also be found in apartments in big cities. No one really knows how many Christians attend those fellowships because they don't keep accurate numbers or records of baptisms. Many Christians who attend a home fellowship will also attend a registered church because they want to worship in a church building. And some Christians who attend a registered church on Sundays will attend a home fellowship during the week; there is quite a bit of overlap, especially in the cities.

Many Chinese Christians have been involved in social projects like establishing kindergartens and providing help for the poor. This is coordinated through the Amity Foundation, founded by the China Christian Council. The Amity Foundation has over 1,000 programs, such as community development, water projects, and welfare projects. The Church considers this Foundation very important, since it helps to change the image of the Church in society so that people don't see only evangelism and other church-based ministry. Social service reveals that the Church is an organization which serves society.

An example of the tremendous church growth in China is found in Hangzhou, Zhejiang province. The Chong Yi Church had 2,000 members when it dedicated its new church building in 2005. Today, it has thousands of baptized believers. It holds two services each Sunday with a total attendance of more than 10,000. The building is currently the largest church building in China. The senior pastor Rev. Gu told us that over 800 new converts were baptized in 2012, and in the past eight years 5,200 baptisms were held in his church. For the past three years, the number of baptisms has been increasing by about one-hundred each year. God is moving in the Church in China in an astonishing way today.

CHAPTER 2

China's fate

Three centuries ago, China began to experience a devastating upheaval not suffered before.

In the period from 1775 until 1839 China was in decline. The phenomenal explosion of its population was part of the reason for its demise. Farmers were unable to provide enough food to feed the masses. For instance, within one century (between 1700 and 1800) the population exploded from 138 to 342 million. By 1850 it reached 412 million! New technologies, then used in Europe, were at that time often not accepted by unadventurous Emperors of the Qing Dynasty (1644-1911). This was a huge problem for them! They should have been more vigilant and forward-looking in this instance. The results were disastrous.

People began to die of starvation; only the fittest and those with special privileges survived. It was a sad period for a proud nation. Once known as the largest and most advanced nation in the world, became one of the poorest. Those were woeful days.

Corruption was an added reason for its decline, but more than that, an outside force brought total collapse. Britain had smuggled opium into the country from its controlled territory of Bengal. In the period of 1838/39 alone, the British merchants shipped 400 000 crates full of opium into the country—representing 5.6 million pounds.

This infested a vast portion of Chinese people and also diminished the fortitude and resilience of its army. It is believed that at that time ten percent of the Chinese smoked opium and five percent became dreadfully addicted to it. This translates into 41 million and 20 million people respectively, who lived under a contaminating cloud of opium. No wonder for the decline of Chinese civilization!

Finally, in 1838 the Emperor Mianning (also named Daoguang Emperor, 1782-1850) tried to bring an end to this disaster. He sent his special ambassador Lin Zexu to Canton (now known as Guangzhou) to confront not only the Chinese culprits, but also the British authorities to renounce their participation in this evil trade. He succeeded by destroying 1400 tons of opium which had been under British control. Sadly, following this, the enraged British authorities retaliated and began the infamous opium war of 1839-42, which the unprepared and much weaker Chinese troops were not able to win. They capitulated and were humiliated by signing the Unfair Treaty of Nanjing (1842). China was forced to open the cities of Guangzhou, Xiamen, Fuzhou, Ningbo and Shanghai for trade.

However, a much more serious setback for them was to hand over Hong Kong (meaning Fragrant Harbor) to become a British colony. On January 26, 1841 British troops raised the Union Jack in that poor fishing village with only 7,500 inhabitants. Following this, Britain ruled this Chinese territory for 156 years and developed it into a mega-metropolis with 7 million inhabitants, rivaling Berlin, London or New York in its importance.

The above mentioned events resulted in what is now known as The Century of Humiliation for the Chinese. But then everything changed overnight on July 1, 1997. The now famous handover took place, when Hong Kong reverted back to the rule of the Chinese government in Beijing.

Hong Kong truly is an amazing city, as it has been said, "where East meets West". It also considers itself as the "entertainment hub." It boasts 1,223 skyscrapers, and according to the number one provider of building data *Emporis*, it has more buildings over 500 feet (150 m) than any other city, and is one of the most populated city in the world. The earliest recorded European visitor was a Portuguese Jorge Alveres. As an explorer he visited the island in 1513. In the 19th and 20th centuries it developed into what it is now one of the most captivating city anywhere. It is a huge trading center; it is the third international banking center of the world; it houses more international companies than most world cities; it is after the USA the largest movie exporter; and it has some of the world's best hotels and restaurants. Hong Kong has also attracted more tourists than any other city its size.

On the day of the handover I sat in my Hong Kong hotel room to watch the transfer back to China. Present were the Chinese President Jiang Zemin and Prince Charles with Prime Minister Blair representing Great Britain. The British flag was lowered and replaced with the Chinese at the exact stroke of midnight. The Chinese exploded with sheer joy. I have never heard such a voluminous cheer as I heard on that fateful night, when millions of Chinese raised their voices in enthusiastic and overwrought jubilation. As Mao Zedong had promised, China had stood up. The Chinese were ecstatic.

From that time on, the Communists began to rule Hong Kong as part of China. Even though freed from foreign powers, China now was facing a new problem, being subjugated by a different ruler—its own dictator—and a cruel one at that. A large portrait of this despot, namely Mao Zedong, now hangs on the wall of the Tian-an-men Square (Heavenly Peace Square) in Beijing. It is believed that under his brutal reign from 1949-1976, up to 70 million died an abnormal death, either by execution or starvation. In spite of this horrendous record, he is now revered by most Chinese as their Great Chairman. Why so? There are two reasons. For one, the Communist Party has over the past few years morphed into an acceptable and engaging organization, which the people now can willingly embrace. They are ready to forgive and forget the past. Secondly, the Chinese are known for being very patriotic. After all, China has an enduring civilization that lasted at least six millennia. Even today, many Chinese still believe that their country deserves to be seen as the center of the world. A marked spot on the Beijing Tian-an-men Square signifies this reality. To them China is exceptional and irreplaceable.

We will discuss this further in the next few chapters.

CHAPTER 3

China's Fourth Generation

All of us working in China today are facing new challenges. These challenges are God-given and worth accepting. As I look back to my China involvement, I praise God for the many wonderful and meaningful working relationships we have had with our Christian brothers and sisters there. The name of our organization China Partner truly reflects the partnership we experience. We have gone to serve the church in China—we did not go with our own agenda. The need of training emerging young Christian leaders was put before us as a challenge—and this came from the Chinese church leadership. We accepted it. I shall never forget the words of the late Bishop Ting to me so many years ago, "Let's try it; let's do it."

I witnessed dramatic changes within the last twenty-eight years. On my first visit in 1981, I found China to be the same as I had left it in 1949. Now you see the handiwork of competent engineers, architects and businesspersons everywhere. This is amazing! Remember, China is the largest county of the world with its 1.33 billion inhabitants. It has the longest wall, the tallest hotel, the largest city (Chongqing with 32 million), the fastest growing economy, the speediest train (the German Transrapid), and it has the fastest growing church. Furthermore, China now prints more Bibles than any other country in the world. Since 1987, over 105 million rolled off its presses.

Many in the West have asked me how this was made possible with a Communist Government in control. This is a legitimate question after seeing the demise of the Soviet Union and the hardship other communist countries face. However, China is different. It has a six-thousand year history and knows how to cope with many different scenarios.

Since the founding of the People's Republic of China in 1949, the government has experienced numerous changes, also in religious matters.

For instance, in December 2007 Hu Jintao declared a bold shift in China's religious policy. In an unprecedented Politburo session he acknowledged," The knowledge and strength of religious people must be mustered to build a prosperous society." He signaled a move from atheism to secularism—from "no God" to "a non-political role for God."

As we all know by now, there are two major factions of the church in China—the registered church and the non-registered church. I am often asked about the validity of the registered church. Some have the wrong concept or opinion in believing that true Christian believers can only be found in the non-registered Church, the so-called house churches. That is wrong. After having traveled and ministered all across China since 1981, I learned that the millions of Christians in the registered churches are also evangelical, Bible centered and true followers of Jesus. Those from the West working with the registered church, however, have to be open, transparent, honest and legal in all of their activities. This is what we in China Partner have chosen to do. Because of this openness, and in spite of mistakes we have made in the process, we have enjoyed a wonderful togetherness with our Christian friends all over China.

Some evangelical leaders in the West share the concern of most evangelical leaders in China, that liberal theology is making a slow and carefully orchestrated inroad into its churches. However, we must be cautious and tread gently with criticism. The Chinese Church is presently seeking its own identity. Repeatedly I was told by many of my friends in China that they have the right to have a Chinese church just like the Europeans have the right to have a European Church, the Americans to have an American church, and the Africans to have an African Church.

Rev. Cao Shengjie, the former General Secretary of the China Christian Council writes, "We believe that the Bible is the revelation from God, the highest authority of faith. Our faith, based on the tenets of the Apostles Creed and the Nicene Creed, will never change." She continues, "Our theological thinking will be based on biblical teaching, historical church tradition and our unique experience of the church and our culture. We hope our efforts will help in the all-around up building of our church and make some contribution to the church universal."

The church organization across China is set up on different levels. There is the leadership of local churches in villages and towns; the leadership on the county level; the leadership on the provincial level; and the leadership on the national level. Time will tell how the church in China will face the challenges of unorthodox theology. Remember, we in the West also had to go through such confrontations. The danger for the church in China does not come from the Chinese political government, as so many in the western world believe; the danger might come from within the church, as was experienced in the West. All the persecution during the Cultural Revolution, and some of it thereafter, when local cadres refused to abide by the new government's religious freedom policies, did not harm the church in its outreach—it strengthened it. This, by the way, is not only unique to China but also to any church worldwide. However, liberal teachings from within the church will be disastrous, as we have seen in so many western churches, especially those in Europe. Liberal theology emptied its churches there.

In addition, this is where we as Bible-believing Christians from outside can serve. We from China Partner are committed to stand shoulder to shoulder with our biblically grounded Chinese brothers and sisters in Christ who work openly and legally. We dare not let them down now! We will continue to fellowship with them. We will listen to their concerns. We will answer their calls if help is needed and desired. We will teach or preach when called upon. We are asking the Lord to give us wisdom as we pursue the path He has put us on. However, we will never interfere with their program, plans or rightful agenda.

How can we help? Get involved in the construction of Bible schools and churches. Ship in sound biblical study books the legal way. Help in the training of emerging young leaders. Encourage those in leadership position to stay true to the Word of God. Sign up for one year to teach English in theological schools. In addition, pray like so many of us have done.

CHAPTER 4

God's amazing work in China

China certainly has been the focus of attention on many occasions. Just to name a few: Tibet, Olympics, earthquakes, and floods. Also, China is the world's most populous country. Its size, combined with a state controlled media, result in events being viewed from different and distinctive perspectives, whether political, economic, cultural or religious. Let us for now focus on the religious.

Did you know that the United Bible Society prints more Bibles in China today than in any other country of the world? In fact, China even exports Bibles! India and some African countries are the beneficiaries. Recently I preached at a church in Hangzhou, a beautiful city a little south of Shanghai. When I asked for a show of Bibles, over two thousand hands went up, each one holding a Bible. Christians in other countries, especially in Europe, where Bibles are usually not taken to church, can learn from this. It was an incredible sight. Just remember, several years back, Bibles were not allowed in China! Christians were put into prison for having Bibles or when sharing with non-believers the gospel of Jesus Christ. However, today it is different. Times truly have changed.

In the early parts of missionary endeavor to China, and right up to the Communist take-over in 1949, missionaries had continuously encountered many obstacles.

However, I along with my son Erik and daughter Linda, now have the privilege to carry on the ministry my parents had to interrupt, when they were forced to leave China after the Communists had taken over China. And that without any hindrance. Over the past few years, we have taken teams into China to teach evangelism and pastoral care courses in theological seminaries and Bible schools across that vast land. We continue to distribute mini-libraries containing Christian volumes wherever we teach. So far, we have shipped books to China worth hundreds of thousands of dollars

At one of China's twenty-three theological seminaries and Bible schools, located in the city of Wuhan in Hubei province, close to two-hundred students prepare themselves for full-time ministries at any given time. They have a deep passion to share Christ with others. The government does not allow Christians to openly share Christ by holding street meetings or passing out tracts on the streets. So what do they do? They wear bright blue jackets with JESUS LOVES YOU emblazoned on the back—both in English and in Chinese. In another city, I saw Christian young people boldly displaying T-shirts with the inscription JESUS IS THE WAY, THE TRUTH, AND THE LIFE.

In one of the most northern provinces of China, Liaoning, where our China Partner team taught at the seminary in the large industrial city of Shenyang, I again had the privilege to preach in one of the churches. Our team arrived for the church's third worship service of that day—they hold five such services each Sunday. Over 2,000 people were jammed into that church, and what a thrill to hear them sing some of the well-known gospel songs. I preached on the subject of 'prayer.' Christians in China love to pray and want to learn how to become better at that. They also love their Bibles.

This church has an amazing story! When that particular church re-opened in 1980, they had an attendance of 220 people. Today the church has grown to over 20,000 members. Since they can only accommodate 10,000 of their church members on any given Sunday in their five services, the other 10,000 have to worship in house churches. They take turns. Those 10,000 members, who had to go to the house churches on one Sunday, will be allowed to attend church the following Sunday. The pastor told me that he had to preach the same sermon at each of the five services, otherwise the people would stay for all services, because they do not want to miss out on anything that is being taught. That is the only way to accommodate all of the members and visitors!

On Wednesday morning, we were taken to a country church. When we arrived at eleven o'clock, about 800 people were jammed into the church building, and hundreds of others sat outside or in side rooms. This is their weekly Wednesday morning Bible study! When we were asked to say a word of greeting, people actually had to be moved out of the church in order for us to be able to get inside!

Mrs. Xie is the wife of a professor of one of the four elite universities in China, located in Wuhan on the mighty river Yangtze. She was thirty-five years old and teaches English at that university. As a teenager, she had read a 'saying' or a quote by Jesus Christ and was so moved by what she read, that she always wanted to find out, who Jesus Christ really is. After giving a lecture at that university, I told the hundreds of university students that had crowded into two lecture halls, "Get a Bible if you want to know more about Jesus Christ." Mrs. Xie was among the listeners, she purchased a Bible and soon after that lecture, she found Christ.

A year later, when telling me the story of her conversion she said, "I am so unworthy of what Christ has done for me." Then her voice broke and as tears filled her eyes, she whispered again, "I am so unworthy."

When people ask me, "Why are the churches in China growing so rapidly?" all I can say is that the Holy Spirit is doing His work, and that in an unusual way. This, of course, also had happened in other countries in years gone by. As we look into history, we know of revivals in many parts of the world. For instance, in Germany revival broke out amongst the Herrenhuter people, which resulted in a thriving mission movement under the leadership of Count Zinzendorf that swept across the world. Or take the Welsh revivals in Great Britain, or the revivals in North America, Indonesia and Korea! But now God has singled out China for revival, and the Gospel is sweeping across the nation as has never happened before.

While teaching at the seminary in Wuhan, which is also used as a distribution center for Bibles in that region, one of the local universities—mind you, those are secular, Marxist dominated universities—had ordered 500 Bibles for their students. Two days later, they upped the order to 1,000 Bibles! What incredible interest to know more about the living God!

In that same city, I was invited by the president emeritus of one of the universities to meet him for lunch. As a young man, while studying at one of the universities in Eastern China, he had run across some Christians, but decided to become a Marxist. The teachings of Karl Marx had gripped the minds of the young intellectuals of his day. But now, sitting across from me at the lunch table, he shared with me his conviction that the Christian faith has something to offer to Chinese society. He started an "Institute for Studies on Christianity," and it already had over 1,000 students. The government in Beijing had approved this institute. He asked me to help him find lecturers from overseas who could lecture on Christianity at his new founded institute. Of course, it was my desire to find those that are of evangelical and biblical persuasion. I am now looking for evangelical professors who can go to Wuhan for short-term or even long-term sessions.

Before teaching at the seminaries, we always do some singing. The Chinese students love to sing. While this happened in one of the seminaries where we taught, a young man passing by on the street, heard the singing and came inside wanting to know what this was all about. He was introduced to one of the seminary students, who a few minutes later led him to Christ.

Thousands of young university and college students are interested in the gospel. In a major city of China, over 500 of such students came to church after the pastor had dismissed the congregation following a Christmas Eve service. The students wanted to know more about Jesus Christ, so the pastor and the seminary students shared the gospel with them. Several of those students became Christians that night, and most of the others stayed until 5 o'clock in the morning to know more about the Savior.

This is the new China. China is rapidly changing. As the country rushes to industrialize and improve its economy, official attitudes are changing. Christianity no longer is denounced as the opiate of society. Intellectuals are more open to the Gospel than any time since 1949. The Bible is even used as a study topic in some universities.

The church in China has virtually exploded in the last forty years.

However, this rapid growth has left a leadership gap. Only a few thousand ordained ministers, many of them elderly, serve these churches, and new leaders are not being trained fast enough to keep up. Their monthly income averages less than a day's pay in much of the West. It is here, in the area of preparing and equipping future Christian leaders, that our ministry is making its greatest contribution.

As I stated above, twenty-three theological seminaries and Bible schools now exist in China. Furthermore, regional schools for resident short-term study by lay leaders, and evening courses in the cities now train church workers. The theological seminaries and Bible schools have graduated thousands of students since the Cultural Revolution; over 1,800 students are enrolled each year. 61 percent of seminary teachers are recent graduates of those schools. However, hampered by lack of facilities, funds, and other resources, the schools can accommodate fewer than half of those who apply.

We of China Partner try to build bridges of friendship, understanding and communication. We relay accurate information about the church in China. This is so Christians in the West can know better how to pray, help and participate with their Chinese brothers and sisters in efforts to reach all of China for Christ.

When I had the privilege to preach in one of the cities, Nanchang, where my parents had done missionary work so many years ago, hundreds of people could not get into the overcrowded church. Those in the churchyard listened to the message over loudspeakers, and when, after the message, I made my way through the crowd standing outside, I felt a tug at my coat. It was the young pastor of that church, and he said: "Lin Musse—my name in Chinese—, turn around, and look at those people. This is the fruit of your parents, and the fruit of the other missionaries who labored here so many years ago." I was deeply moved, knowing that my parents had often been so discouraged. I wished so much for them to see this for themselves, but they are already in heaven. Then I raised my face to heaven and said: "Thank you, father, thank you, mother, for having stayed faithful to God's call, and for having remained in China to preach the gospel to the Chinese people. I want so badly to have you with me here now! If you could only see the fruit of your toils, hardships, and disappointments! Thank you, father, and thank you, mother."

CHAPTER 5

Christianity in the People's Republic of China

Many conflicting reports come out of China these days. A careful observer has to take many things into account before making an intelligent assessment or even judgment about the religious scene in China now.

China is a multi-religious country. Buddhism, Islam, Taoism and Christianity are the main religions. Confucianism is more of a *Weltanschauung* or a philosophy for a way of life. The government propagates atheism. A government agency, the Religious Affairs Bureau (RAB now State Administration of Religious Affairs, SARA), does not control but rather supervises all religious activities in China.

Over the last few years, Christianity has made significant inroads into the minds and hearts of the Chinese people. It has become one of the major religions in China. On my close to ninety-five trips into China since 1981, I have concentrated my studies and research on the development of the mainline Chinese Christian church, represented by the China Christian Council.

The early Christian beginnings in China can be traced to the Nestorians during the Tang Dynasty in A.D. 635. By 1368, they disappeared from the China scene. Franciscans and Jesuits were the next Christian groups to move into China. Matteo Ricci, a brilliant

Jesuit, established his residence in Beijing in 1601. He, and the Jesuits who followed, adapted Christianity to some Chinese customs.

Robert Morrison was the first Protestant missionary to China. He settled in Guangzhou (formerly Canton) in 1807. Within twelve years, he had translated the Bible into Chinese.

The Chinese developed great resentments against abrasive foreigners. Military interventions followed, but foreign powers always won the upper hand. A number of infamous "unequal treaties" were signed, the first of which was signed in Nanjing in 1842.

Missionaries from then on enjoyed the protection of those treaties that actually had been set up to legalize foreign trade. The worst aspects of the treaties were the toleration clauses, which granted Christian converts the protection of foreign laws. This did not sit well with the Chinese nor, eventually, with many of the missionaries. After 1925, most mission boards urged that those special privileges should cease.

It is interesting to note that the father of the Chinese Revolution in 1911 was a Christian. On numerous occasions, Dr. Sun Yat-sen attempted to establish a Republic. He finally succeeded, and, in Wuhan on October 10, 1911, the first republic in China was introduced. A large and beautiful mausoleum was built in his honor in Nanjing. Even the Communists revere him today.

Protestant missionary activities were quite impressive. Besides making converts, they established many charitable and educational institutions such as hospitals, clinics, orphanages, homes and schools for the blind, retirement homes, mission schools, colleges, and universities. By 1915, Protestant missions had 330 hospitals and 223 dispensaries serving 1,640,259 patients. However, in spite of all their good works, the missionaries had not been able to rid themselves of the taint of foreign domination. Christianity was still a foreign religion, and foreigners, rather than any distinctive Christian dogma or practice, made it offensive.

Even though foreign missionaries have had as their goal to

build an indigenous church, it was difficult for them to let go. The ordination of native pastors was a slow process. In addition, the Chinese Christians could not shoulder the financial upkeep of the many "sophisticated" institutions. The Chinese church depended heavily upon foreign aid.

By 1926, 8,325 Protestant missionaries labored in China. They represented many denominational and interdenominational mission boards. The China Inland Mission, founded by Hudson Taylor, was one of the largest.

The Revolution in 1911 brought about a strong feeling of nationalism. This was a healthy development for China but had its bearing on missionary work and the church in China.

One of the most nationalistic forces grew out of a tiny beginning of the Chinese Communist Party (CCP). In 1921, the Communist Party was founded in Shanghai. Twelve Chinese, mostly young men, were present. One of them was Mao Zedong, a native of Hunan. He was born in 1893 in the village of Shao Shan, forty miles from the provincial capital Changsha. His father was a farmer, and after his primary schooling, he helped his father on the farm. Then he pursued further studies in Changsha before going to Beijing, where he worked as a librarian. It was there where he first read the Communist Manifesto and became an ardent Marxist.

The political party Kuomintang (KMT), founded by Sun Yat-sen, had its hands full fighting off warlords in the period from 1912-27. As the Communist Party developed in strength, the KMT under Chiang Kai-shek had to concentrate meeting this new threat. Mao retreated to the province of Jiangxi, where he established the first Chinese Soviet republic. Chiang Kai-shek then organized four extermination campaigns, but all of them failed.

One of the greatest feats of the Communist Party was the Long March, which began in Jiangxi and ended in the Northwestern province of Shaanxi. They passed through eleven provinces, traversed eighteen mountain ranges, and crossed twenty-four rivers, including the Tatu gorge and the mighty Yangtze. But the human toll was enormous. It is believed that out of 100,000 men and women, only 10,000 made it to Shaanxi.

The key lessons Mao learned on this trek was the identification with the peasants and the principles of guerilla warfare. His whole regime was later built on his empathy towards the peasantry. He learned how to live with them, how to think like them, and how to organize them.

When Mao finally took control of China in 1949, he had to deal with religion. As an atheist, he felt that religion was a thing of the past and therefore not needed. The Chinese Christians had to come to terms with this new development, and this was not easy.

However, religious freedom was guaranteed in the 1954 Constitution but mostly not heeded. Initially Mao thought that religion would fade away by itself. But it did not. Sterner measures were introduced to hamper the propagation of the Christian faith (and other religious beliefs, as well).

Christianity was viewed with a greater degree of antagonism and suspicion because of its historical links with the Western powers that had oppressed China, and with the capitalistic system that apparently had exploited the people. The relationships Christians had with foreign missionaries became a severe detriment.

There were two options left to the Christians. They could accommodate or go "underground". Some of the leaders opted for the first one. They met with the government in Beijing to hammer out accepted policies. At first liberal and conservative Christians worked hand in hand but later this coalition broke apart.

Some of the Christian leaders produced a document addressing foreign mission boards. In it, they spelled out the fact that changes were necessary in light of the new historical developments in China. The document was kind and friendly in tone, but decisive in content. There was no way that foreign missions or churches should have any control over the church in China.

The Three Self Patriotic Movement (TSPM) was founded in the early 50s. Many of the leaders were theologically liberal. Many of the evangelical leaders were not willing to cooperate. They continued to minister in "underground", whereas the TSPM was able to function openly and that quite well. Only during the Cultural Revolution, all churches were closed. Persecution on a grand scale set in. Many pastors and Christian leaders were sent into labor camps. They were forced to do menial labor. Some experienced the martyr's death.

With the death of Mao, certain freedoms were reintroduced. The Chinese Christians call this "relative freedom." In 1979, the first church (in Ningbo) was reopened and hundreds followed suit. In the meantime, millions have joined the ranks of Christians in the approved, thus legal churches.

The Amity Press in Nanjing has printed over 105 million Bibles since 1987. By adding more sophisticated printing presses on a new site, it now has the potential of printing up to twelve million Bibles each year.

I am optimistic about the future of the church in China. God has not closed the chapter on China.

CHAPTER 6

A President's True Identity

With his chapter I want to shift gears. I want to compare some of the Chinese government leaders with someone in the western world, who in my mind is an outstanding Christian. These are some of my thoughts regarding a much maligned President of the United States. Reading now, what I had written some time ago about George W. Bush and his amazing presidency, makes me realize how mean and wrong the mass media can be. As Christians we ought to be involved in civic events. The Bible admonishes us to pray for our political leaders, whether we agree or don't agree with their policies. I often said, "If God had not predestined me to become a man of the cloth, I would have become a politician." That is why I feel compelled to put it in this book.

So this is what I wrote many years ago:

I am used to distorted media reports, but I have never heard such vicious, slanderous, hateful, deceitful, untrue, warped and misleading reporting as was done ever since President George W. Bush was elected President of the United States—and especially about him.

As a German citizen living in the United States, I always tried to be fair and report honestly about the events taking place in this country. Many don't realize that a remarkable battle for the American mind is presently being waged. Issues such as abortion (especially partial birth abortion), stem cell research, gay rights and same sex marriages are constantly and forcefully debated all across the country. This has split the country into two major factions. As committed Christians we, of course, take a biblical stand on these issues.

You will notice that those are moral issues. Hollywood and the bulk of its supporters are in the one camp and most of evangelical Christians are in the other. Since everyone living in this country has a right to his or her own opinion, it is understandable that the media will take advantage of this and will do everything in its power to stir up the people to a hyped frenzy. The more they do this, the more money they will make. And in America the bottom line is king.

Let me explain some of the differences between European and American culture.

But listen first to how the director of the German polling group Infratest assesses the difference between European and American culture and comes to this conclusion: "It would be problematic in Germany today for a politician to present him/herself as a devout Christian in the way that President George W. Bush does in America." So in Europe it is about religion! To them devout Christians are suspect just because they follow the teachings of Jesus Christ.

Interestingly, to those who study the life of President Bush carefully, must admit that he does not carry his faith on his sleeves. So people cannot fault him for that. What they do see, however, is his decent lifestyle. He does not lie, nor cheat, nor mislead, nor slander, nor abuse alcohol—which, by the way, he did as a young man—nor does he carouse around, and above all, he does not womanize like so many politicians have done and still do. In other words he illustrates his faith more by deeds than by words.

Europe is a secular society. Religion does not play as great a role there as it does in the United States. Church membership has been on the decline for decades. Church buildings are constantly being closed down and used for secular enterprises. Some heads of state refuse to recite "so help me God" while being sworn in. Pornography is widely propagated openly in magazines and on TV. Europe as a whole has become a pagan continent. The "God is dead" movement has taken its toll in the minds and behavior of the majority of Europeans. Church attendance is at an all-time low. Less than 5% of Europe's population is worshipping in its gorgeous edifices. Churches and cathedrals have become tourist sites; they are no longer true worship centers.

The United States is somewhat different. Even though many Americans are somewhat following the European trend, there are still multitudes that are outspoken about their Christian belief. Foreigners visiting the United States are always amazed to see churches "on every street corner." The vast majority of its citizens believe in God—over eighty percent! An estimated thirty percent or more are evangelical Christians—those that believe in a personal God and who have accepted Jesus Christ as Lord and Savior. It is true that many Christians are shallow in their beliefs; however, they still marshal the backbone of basic Christian values.

This the Europeans and especially the mass media in Europe cannot and does not want to accept. When the Americans reelected President Bush, the media went ballistic. For months before the election journalists painted a distorted picture of the President and embraced Senator Kerry as "their candidate." They desperately wanted him to win. Bush stood for biblical values; Kerry did not.

Most of them did not do what journalists are supposed to do, that of reporting facts fairly and honestly. They deliberately tried to persuade their readers that Bush is bad and consequently Kerry would win. At least they hoped so. But then they were proven wrong, and mightily so. When reality finally set in, they simply could not understand that Americans would prefer Bush over Kerry. And that with an amazing majority. Never before in US history have so many people voted for a president. When Kennedy won over Nixon it was only done with a little over 100,000 votes. Clinton did not even reach forty-five percent of the popular vote. But Bush beat Kerry with more than 3.5 million votes and won fifty-two percent of the popular vote.

This was an astounding accomplishment and victory. "How can that many Americans be so dumb," European pundits thought, and some even had the audacity to express this in their columns.

This to me shows two things: Firstly, it portrays the arrogance of European journalists, and secondly the total ignorance of the press when it comes to reading the minds of American citizens. Now, it would not be so bad if the journalists would keep their nonsense to themselves, but with their biased reporting they influence and poison the minds of millions of people. The mass media around the world is responsible for fanning the hatred towards the US president and with it towards America.

This is exactly what they have done to the Europeans. Let me explain further.

However, I want to concentrate my observations on Germany. As a German I don't want to throw contempt on other nationalities. Those in error and especially those who publicized lies and innuendos in other countries will have to be dealt with by their own people. Like the Frenchman who published a book in which he alleges that President Bush orchestrated the 9/11 incident. Among other lies he stated that Bush ordered an American missile to hit the Pentagon. When the author was confronted with the question where all the dead passengers now are, he answered appallingly, "President Bush has much to answer for." He sold close to one million copies of his book! And people believe his deranged reasoning. And that in so-called enlightened Europe!

Whenever I traveled through my home country Germany over the last few years, I was stunned to hear and see what was reported on the radio and on television. But what was worse were the reports in newspapers and magazines. What you hear and see on radio and TV you may more readily forget, but what you read will leave a lasting imprint on your mind. I thought I was reliving the days of Nazism with its goebbelized propaganda. The innuendos, lies and vicious attacks on President Bush were nauseating.

Have you ever heard of Ted Turner? He is one of the US media moguls. He grew up in Christian surroundings but later radically turned against God. As a successful media man he once declared: "Christians are losers." He has total disregard for any person with Christian beliefs, and since President Bush is a committed Christian, he will come under his attack. Other liberal journalists do the same thing.

Have you heard of Dan Rather's debacle? As the famous news anchorman for CBS News, he tried to smear President Bush during the election campaign. He used forged documents to "prove" Bush's failure when he served in the National Guard (Air Force). Rather had to resign in disgrace.

Why is it that Bush-hating has become so prevalent in Europe and among liberals in the United States? Why do so many totally misunderstand and misinterpret him and with it his policies?

Let me first state who he is.

President Bush was born into a noble, prominent, honorable and successful family. His father had been president of the United States. He studied at two prestigious universities: Harvard and Yale. As a young man he was easy going and prone to drinking too much alcohol. He married a God-fearing girl, who helped him to overcome his drinking problem. Later he met Billy Graham who made him consider accepting Christ as his Savior. During the presidential campaign a journalist asked both Bush and Kerry to share about their faith. Kerry refused several times, but Bush published his written testimony. Here is an excerpt:

> "The seeds of my decision [to follow Christ, ed.] had been planted by the Reverend Billy Graham. It was the beginning of a new walk where I would commit my heart to Jesus Christ."

President Bush has learned through personal experiences how important it is to find forgiveness and rest in Jesus. The President has become a disciplined man and he takes care of his body. He jogs and/or spends time in the fitness center. He goes to bed around 9:00 pm to get a good night's rest and gets up around 5:30 in the morning.

He has become a spiritual man. He begins his day with personal devotions. He reads through the Bible once every two years. He studies devotional books like "My Utmost for the Highest" by Oswald Chambers. He is a man of prayer and often opens his cabinet meetings with prayer.

He is a compassionate man. He is involved in efforts to advance his agenda of compassionate conservatism such as his "No Child Left Behind" plan or his "Aids Recovery" funding program.

He is a decisive man. In his first term he has proven to follow through with what he set out to do. Before making a decision he listens to competent counselors and once his mind is made up he moves. Kerry was just the opposite. TIME described Kerry well: "… [he] renovated virtually every position he had ever taken and shook the grave dust off his suit several times before arriving at history's door…he was guided by no core beliefs but was only searching for a politically safe place to land." Kerry was a "waffler," President Bush was and is not.

He is an honest man. This is so refreshing, because the last US president did not only mislead the American people but also lied under oath. Can you imagine a president lying under oath? Recent polls show that less than ten percent of Americans now think Clinton was a good president. They did not trust him then and they just don't trust him now. It is a mystery to many of us that Europeans in general think highly of him. They apparently do not mind for a person holding the highest and most prestigious office in the United States, to drop his pants in the Oval Office quarters while being "serviced" by a White House girl intern, and then to lying about it.

And then to hear about the accolades Michael Moore received at the Cannes Festival was mind-boggling! For Europeans to be duped by such a charlatan is amusing to Americans. Don't they realize that it has been proven that forty-nine of the incidents he describes in his so called "documentary" are misinterpretations and even lies? We thought that Europeans are more sophisticated and would be able to distinguish between fact and fiction. But obviously many Europeans have been so brainwashed by the media that they are incapable of making sound judgments, and thus are willing to sacrifice their own honor and reputation on the altar of deceit. And watch out, the liberal press will continue to protect Moore. The Hollywood crowd may even try to "honor" him with an Oscar nomination. Don't forget, however, that the Hollywood elite is made up of people who dislike Christians and are known for salacious life styles—not an honorable way to live.

Let us get back to President Bush. He proved to the American public and to fair-minded people around the world that he is worthy of their trust. In spite of the disdain shown by the majority of the world's population, there are those who are grateful to him. When nations were asked how they rate the President, most of them, after having been influenced by distorted press reports, were unfavorable— except Iraq and a couple of other nations. In Iraq only terrorists and criminals side with those in the world who hate him. Remember how the press called him a liar? It was not he who lied; the real liars were those who labeled him a liar, because doing so was the greatest lie. President Bush does not lie and did not lie about Iraq or anything else.

The vast majority in Iraq are grateful that they have been liberated by the American-led coalition. Critics who say the opposite just don't get it. After all, the Iraqis are the ones who suffered under the brutal regime of Sadam Hussein. They are the ones who had over 300,000 of their loved ones buried in mass graves. They are the ones who saw their neighbors and relatives with tongues cut out, ears cut off, hands hacked off and some of them fed to shredders. They are the ones who are grateful. I shall never forget the happy and thankful smiles on the faces of seven Iraqis showing off their new prosthetic hands while visiting the President in the White House. Of course there are difficulties in Iraq, but those are not caused by the general public, nor are they caused by coalition forces; they are caused by terrorists and criminals.

By the way, many Americans still do not understand how some Europeans, especially the French and the Germans, were grateful to accept the sacrifices of over 300,000 American soldiers who gave their lives to liberate their nations in 1945, but could not bring themselves to stand shoulder to shoulder with their former liberators, when they set out once again to liberate another oppressed country. It seems that the Germans always prefer to be on the wrong side when war is the last resort in solving the world's problems. This was so in the First World War and again in the Second World War (to be accurate, even some of the French were on the wrong side—those around Marshal Petain). It seems that only the British and other nationalities like the Dutch, the Danes, the Polish, the Australians, and the Japanese—just to name a few—are the ones who truly understand what it means to help others to experience true freedom. Those were the ones who turned out to be real and faithful friends.

Many blame President Bush to have started the war against Iraq without legitimacy and without the approval of the United Nations. Seventeen UN resolutions failed to rein in Sadam Hussein. The UN turned out to be just a debating club. After months of failed effort to get the Security Council take final action, President Bush along with thirty plus nations decided to oust Sadam Hussein. Was this legitimate?

Well, was it legitimate to have a despot imprison innocent people, torture them beyond description, enjoy rape rooms, throw people down high buildings, cut out tongues, chop off limbs, gas his own people with weapons of mass destruction, execute hundreds of thousands and bury them in mass graves? This he did for thirty years. Where have been the millions of demonstrators around the world during that time, and where were the journalists and politicians with their denunciations? Where were the world leaders, and where was the world body United Nations to take action against such atrocities and oust that tyrant? The UN failed with the Rwanda disaster and is again failing in Sudan.

Some say the Iraq controversy was about oil. I agree. But I have a different take on this. As we now know, a number of countries, especially the French and Russians were trying to protect their own business interests in Iraq, and most of them were related to oil. Furthermore, what about the Oil for Food program? This is now under investigation and President Chirac with Mr. Paque, among others, will have to answer many questions regarding kick-backs they are alleged to have received. So does the Secretary General of the United Nations Kofi Anan and his son. Anan was chided by Volker's report on March 29, 2005 for failing to properly oversee the Oil for Food program. The final report will be published in the summer of 2005. His son is under further scrutiny. The biggest scandal in UN's short history is presently being unearthed. No wonder the UN did not support the effort to have Sadam Hussein removed from office. It was about oil—the way they profited by it. Under the eyes of the United Nations 21 billion US dollars have been misused by Sadam Hussein to further his activities of terror. And western businessmen are part of this scandal. It is amazing that the liberal press is trying again to protect the perpetrators by not sharply criticizing those offenders.

By the way, many Europeans supported the war in the Balkans, and I agree; but why was that war acceptable even though there was no approval by the United Nations? Did we not go in there to save further thousands from being slaughtered? What is so different between those two wars?

The question has been asked over and over again why President Bush was re-elected. In the eyes of the voters he is the better man. He sticks to his beliefs and does not pursue policy by polls. He says what he believes, and he believes what he says. He is a normal human being with flaws like all of us. He even makes fun of his problem with the English language. "People sometimes have to correct my

English," he once quipped. "I knew I had a problem when Arnold Schwarzenegger started doing it." But it is so much more important to be a faithful husband and a loving father. It is so much more important to be grounded in faith and pursue a life based on Christian values. It is so much more important to be a fearless leader in the face of ones adversaries. He has become a role model for many because he seems to be so at ease with himself. Criticisms thrown at him don't faze him because he does not have to defend himself. And by the way, false criticisms based on innuendos and lies just don't stick—at least not to him. That's why he won!

President George W. Bush is what he is—a man without guile and a man of great character.

CHAPTER 7

The Heavenly Man: Liu Zhenying, alias Yun

Now I must include a chapter which will edify many people who have been confused and puzzled about this man. For some time I have been asked about the validity of the accounts in his book *The Heavenly Man*. They definitely sound like fairytales. After reading it in depth, I was perplexed and at the same time bemused and bewildered. How is it possible for anyone to make claims like he does! How can anyone after writing such tales keep a straight face!

Let me dive in with my reflections.

Right from the outset, I want to make clear my belief that God is omnipotent and that He does perform miracles even today. If not, why would most churches across the world hold prayer meetings? Participants of such meetings tend to pray for miracles, whether they are for physical healing (Lord, please heal sister Bertha from her bout with cancer), or the salvation of loved ones (Lord, convict my grandson of his need for a Savior).

After reading this controversial book "The Heavenly Man" portraying the experiences and encounters of Mr. Yun, I decided to meet him and his wife in person, so that he could explain his excessive and startling pronouncements. I spent more than two hours with them at the Sheraton Hotel in Frankfurt. I was deeply disturbed by his presentation, not so much for relating his bizarre and outlandish "experiences", but how he did it without a trace of shame or remorse. While still claiming that the statements in his book were true, he neither was able to clarify them in a rational and judicious way, nor could he back them up convincingly. For him to make things more spiritually plausible, he reverts to incidents right out of the Bible, which I will elucidate below. All he could say, when confronted on each issue, was "God performed a miracle." This man came across as being delusional. This brother in Christ has been carried away with his fantasies, and was unashamedly willing to exaggerate beyond reason in order to support and/or plot his imaginations and fancies. Others have expressed harsher verdicts—they call him a liar.

To be fair to him, we must realize that he is a child of the disastrous Cultural Revolution. (1966-76), and thus did not have the opportunity to receive proper education—in fact he told me he hardly had any education at all. Furthermore, he was born into an area in China that is known to be very remote and backward. Folk religions are prevalent there, as in many rural areas across China.

This does not mean that he himself is not intelligent; to the contrary, he obviously is very bright for he was able to mislead even well learned and cultured western Christians. He also states (p. 33 in his book) that he memorized the entire book of Matthew, one chapter a day—and those are long chapters—and that within twenty-eight days! To do this he must be exceptionally smart. Later he memorized supposedly fifty-five chapters—all the chapters from Hebrews to Revelation (p. 180). This is quite remarkable and fascinating to me personally, because as a young man I also had memorized Scripture—the books of Philippians, James and the gospel of John plus hundreds of verses through courses that the Navigators (a well-respected mission organization) recommended. But it took me several years to accomplish this.

After having looked into his eyes and read his body language, I have great doubts that many of his stories are legitimate. No, I would say, many of them are untrue. Let me go through them point by point to expose fabrications and deceptions.

Having been imprisoned—and that in a maximum security prison—how was he able to escape so easily?

> When he told me of this 'miracle', I was reminded of Acts chapters five and twelve. I was impressed with his intimate knowledge of Bible stories, and to be fair to him, I also sensed a **need.** His **need** is to feel accepted by his peers. In order to excel, he quite obviously has to make some of those biblical miracles become his own. He does it by turning them into his personal experiences.

As a young man he lived through a difficult period, and against all odds he wanted desperately to be seen as one totally consumed with serving his Lord—no matter what the cost. On one occasion he felt rebuffed by a pastor of the registered church (TSPM). On page 50 he states:" [I] was even open to the possibility of being a leader for our area if that was what God wanted." Then on page 51 he continues: "More than ninety percent of the delegates wanted me to be chairman of the Christian Association, but a few publicly slandered me, saying I was a false pastor because I had never attended a seminary." In anger, he left the meeting that had been arranged by the RAB (Religious Affairs Bureau) and the PSB (Public Security Bureau) declaring: "Don't you ever invite me to a meeting like this again!"

According to his story, he later was arrested and imprisoned—and that four times! He once broke both of his legs jumping out of a window two-storey high, trying to evade the arrest by several policemen (p. 241). After having been severely beaten and tortured in a maximum-security prison (Zhengzhou Number One Maximum Security Prison) he could only crawl. "Bones snapped," "fractured legs," "crippled legs," "limp legs," that's how he describes his state of affairs at that time. However, suddenly he was healed (p. 259)!

Walking from a solitary confinement cell through three open iron doors and/or gates, his broken yet suddenly healed legs carried him to freedom.

On another occasion, his handcuffs fell off after the Holy Spirit had told him, "Relax your hands" (p. 179). See Acts 12.7

These are stories copied right out the book of Acts.

> *As a registered condemned villain and outlaw to Chinese authorities, how was he able to leave China so easily?*

According to his account the police was looking for him all over, after he had "escaped" from the maximum security prison located in his home province of Henan. Over the years, he had previously been imprisoned on four different occasions, the last of which he had been convicted for a period of fifteen years. In spite of multiple verdicts levied against him over the years, and in spite of him being a dishonorable fugitive in one of the most restricted countries of the world, he alleges to have been able to escape China via Beijing—and that with a false passport, and without difficulties (p. 270-272)!

All of us frequent travelers know that airlines are forbidden to transport people who do not have proper credentials, such as visas. If they fail enforcing this, they pay heavy fines, and the person involved will have to be flown back at the expense of the airline. A friend of his from Vietnam, who had escaped his home country during the period of the so called "boat people calamity", and who had been accepted by Germany as a political refugee, and eventually been extended German citizenship, had given him one of his two German passports. How come he had two passports!

Imagine two passports! As a German citizen I have had experiences in obtaining German passports. The German government does not randomly hand out two passports to the same person, except in an extreme set of circumstances. Only frequent and recurrent overseas travelers, who need visas to enter different countries in quick succession and on a continuous basis, have such a privilege. I know this through personal experience, because I have traveled to over one-hundred-twenty countries. I often needed visas for a number of countries within a short span of time. Only then was I able to receive an additional passport in order for me to get the visas I needed and that only once and for a restricted time.

Without a visa for Germany and with a false passport, which obviously did not carry his name nor his own photo, the Chinese border police at the Beijing airport first challenged him saying, "You are not the person depicted on this photo." However, they let him pass the check point without further ado, and let him leave the country. The same thing allegedly happened at the Frankfurt airport. Again, he was first challenged by the authorities, but then they let him pass. When I interviewed employees of the German border police at the same Frankfurt airport about this case, and asked what they would do with someone who tried to enter the country illegally with a false passport, they responded spontaneously: "We arrest him." When I told them that I had read this in a book where the author actually states that he had experienced this at the Frankfurt airport, I was told: "You

must read 'merkwürdige' (weird or bizarre) literature."

After probing further about his Vietnamese friend, whom I also
wanted to interview, Mr. Yun said, "I don't know where he now
lives—we have 'grown apart' during the last few years." I was not
content with such an explanation and continued to prod more, but he
evaded any further questions.

*How was he able to run from point A to point B within
a "few moments that should have taken hours?"*
(p. 39)

This again comes right out of the Bible, copying the story, where
Philip was physically moved away from a Gaza desert road after
having led the Ethiopian Eunuch to faith in Christ, to a remote place
called Azotus, some 25 miles away. Time and space are eliminated.

*Fasting for seventy-four days and night "without
eating one grain of rice or drinking one drop of
water" (p. 133) is another incredible feat.*

Here Mr.Yun is trying to repeat the fasting of Jesus. He is now
going from the ridiculous to the sublime. Jesus only fasted by not
eating anything. The Bible does not mention Him not drinking any
liquids. "If Jesus can do 40 days and nights without bread then I can
do seventy-four days without even a drop of water," he must have
assumed.

On another occasion not related to Mr. Yun, sadly, a so called
Korean missionary recently serving in Wuhan, taught that only after
forty days of fasting true spirituality can be achieved. Two students
of the theological seminary in Wuhan fell for this trap of misleading
teaching—one of them died on the 36th day, the other soon thereafter.
But Yun alleges to have done it for seventy-four days! Incredible!

How did "the rope behind my back suddenly snap by itself (p. 64)?"

Here he copies Peter's story, when his shackles fell off and an angel let him out of prison. See Acts 12.6-10.

But this is not all. He also alleges to have jumped over an eight-foot wall covered with glass splinters.

How did he do that? "First I pulled up unto the wall as high as I could manage...all of a sudden I felt as if somebody hoisted me up and threw me over. I jumped so far that I even cleared the septic tank"—and a ten-foot-wide open septic tank at that (p. 65)! This he gleaned from Psalm 18.29.

As you go through the book many more strange phenomena, such as visions, dreams and miracles are recounted. I will mention just a few.

"Blind could see, deaf could hear, and lame walked. Christians touched my clothes hoping to receive healing" (p. 193).

Here Mr. Yun copies the stories where Jesus and also some of His disciples encountered such incidents. To be fair, he does not claim he had the same power as Jesus had, but he apparently likes to be seen as someone who is being put on a "higher" pedestal than others. However, when I asked one of the house church pastors in Wenzhou about Mr. Yun and his Wenzhou experiences he said, "I don't know that man nor have I ever heard of him."

He heard a voice...twice went to his mother asking whether she had talked to him..."Go back to sleep," she said (p. 34).

Here he fantasizes to have the experience Samuel had, when awakened by the Lord he rushed to his mentor Eli, who told him to go back to bed and await God's instructions.

> *"Worms started exiting my body through my skin and I itched all over (p. 343).*

> *"Two bottles of IV were injected into my muscle [because the doctor could not find a vein] (p. 114).*

Furthermore, he also makes false statements, such as: "They [Communist authorities] even decree that certain parts of the Bible cannot be preached such as the Second Coming of Christ" (p. 54). I presume that emotionally he still "lives" in times of the Cultural Revolution (1966-76). Many above mentioned harsh restrictions were enforced during that time, but his book was released in 2002 and 2003, many years since the end of that dreadful event and those allegations. It is unfortunate and deplorable that such false accusations are made by him and even worse, that they are then picked up and spread by evangelical Christian leaders of today.

After our long encounter at the Frankfurt airport he closed his deliberations and explanations with a word of prayer. He seemed so spiritual yet came across so fake—a master manipulator. I now understand how people with good intentions can fall for such a man. In a time where so much of Christianity—especially in the western world—is so predictable yet lifeless, spiritually thirsty Christians are looking for exciting miracle stories. Here you have them!

Herein I see the danger. The Benny Hinn's, Jimmy Swaggert's and Reinhardt Bonnke's of our day also attract large crowds and make people believe in miracles, wonders and phenomena that are none.

But what is even more astounding is the fact that some of his counterparts and indigenous house church leaders in China disown him! Their critique of him is stunning and devastating:

"Samuel Lamb (Lin Xiangao) has strongly attacked the 'heavenly man' (Mr. Yun) in a pamphlet several months ago. The two most respected house church leaders in Beijing, Moses Xie and Allen Yuan, have also come out strongly against him. Allen Yuan, who is himself from a Pentecostal background, has said he is a "black sheep disturbing the church".

"In early April 2005 the key leaders of the large rural Sinim Fellowship house churches met in Shanghai and all distanced themselves from Mr. Yun and Peter Xu, whom they regard as heterodox, as they come from the 'Born Again' movement which is widely regarded by most house church leaders in China as extreme, if not downright heretical. Moses Xie has written an article in which he describes how the 'Born Again' evangelists split existing churches with their extreme teaching."

"Mr. Yun has been overseas now for more than seven years, so has Peter Xu. House church leaders in China do not regard them as representative and are unhappy with their activities overseas. The majority of the most respected rural and urban house church leaders have distanced themselves from both Mr. Yun and Peter Xu."

No wonder non-Christians are often disgusted, sickened and then driven away by those who circulate mind-boggling and far-fetched stories. It is my prayer that Christians everywhere will turn again to the foundational teachings of the Bible and examine (Acts 17.11) any queer, sensational or exaggerated tales of those who try to exploit gullible yet sincere believers, thus bringing fame to themselves, but by doing so, dishonor the name of Jesus Christ our Lord

CHAPTER 8

Talk given at the Groundbreaking Ceremony Ningdu, Jiangxi Church

Dear members of the church, officials of the Religious Affairs Bureau, and friends of the church.

What a joy to be present today at the momentous occasion when you lay the foundation of your new church. Many, many years ago I lived with my parents here in Ningdu. I was only a teenager then, but I remember so well the services that were held in the church building you are now about to replace. In fact, I was baptized on this spot. Many warm memories flood into my mind as I see you all assembled here today.

In a way, I am representing my parents who are now in heaven. From above they rejoice with us today. No doubt, they would like to be physically present today. They cannot. However, taking their place I am glad to introduce their grandchildren Erik and Linda and their great-grandchildren Jerusha and Tilon.

God is thrilled when His people move forward in faith. He loves to see them advance the cause of Christ. He is rejoicing when He sees His followers reach out in love to their fellow citizens. Christians are called to love their country and help society fight hunger, poverty and disease. Christians must help in advancing a harmonious society.

God also expects Christians to love their church. God wants his children to love each other. Christians resemble a family. God is our heavenly father and we as Christians are His children. God loves us, we love God and we are encouraged to love His church.

It is my prayer that this church will not only grow in membership but also in deepening its faith and love as they reach out to their community. I hope that I can return when the new church has been built. I want to thank the local authorities for their gracious help in building this church and the church committee for inviting us to take part in this ceremony. May God bless this country, this church and all of you.

CHAPTER 9

The Role of Theological Education for a Changing Church and Society in China

In my Book *Jesus Never Left China* I used much of the same material as you will find in this chapter. However, due to the importance of this issue, I feel urged to repeat some of what I have penned before.

Many years have passed since the reopening of the first church in Ningbo (Zhejiang) in 1979. Since then over 15,000 churches have registered and thereby received permission by local authorities to carry on their diverse and manifold Christian ministries. Presently six churches are being added or opened every single day. Furthermore, between 30,000 and 40,000 groups of believers, who gather at what are called meeting points, affiliated with the Three-self Patriotic Movement (TSPM)/China Christian Council (CCC), are awaiting their turn of registration. Most of those groups meet in homes, public meeting halls or wherever they find room. Most of them are small, but some of them number in the hundreds, even up to 1,000 worshippers or more. This truly is a remarkable development. In Western thinking, there are a minimum of 55,000 recognized churches in China today. This does not include millions of house church Christians.

With the explosion of church growth in China, unprecedented in the history of Christianity, many churches now are in serious trouble.

Due to a lack of competent and biblically trained pastors, churches are prone to fall to heretical teaching. This is especially true in the house church movement. Therefore, the training of emerging young leaders is of utmost importance. Wang Aiming, Vice-President of Nanjing Union Theological Seminary laments, "At present, many grass root churches do not have a theological foundation, and they are far from meeting the demands of the truth of the Gospel. The basic problem is that many evangelists do not appreciate the idea of theology."

Yan Xiyu, former instructor at the Sichuan Theological Seminary writes, "Many co-workers in the church today tire themselves out with busyness; they are like a fire brigade running off to the next place, they lack an overall vision. Of course, there are many reasons why this situation arose, but the poverty of theology is a crucial element. In our church there is to a greater or lesser extent, faith which is Christian in name but not in substance. Just as poverty of thinking can make a person appear shallow, impetuous, and lost, in the same way, poverty of theology will make a church appear foundationless and easily shaken by the winds of heresy."

In the last few years, up to 2013, it seems that Christianity is experiencing the same process of Sinicizing as Buddhism did in the Tang Dynasty (618-906 AD)—mainly during the 7th and 8th Century.

The great need is to improve the quality of theological education by upgrading the faculties. Only one third of them award theological degrees. The curriculum for seminaries has to be improved as well. The goal is to improve education by the year 2015, paying special attention to the demands of liturgy and pastoral care. Our Chinese friends see the functions of theological education to be fourfold: instruction, research, social ministry, and communication of the gospel and biblical truth. Theological education in China plays a vital role in the spiritual development of the mushrooming churches. After the reemergence of the church in China following the catastrophic Cultural Revolution, the emphasis was first placed on opening and renovating church buildings, and reestablishing theological training centers such as seminaries and Bible schools. In those early years, theology was mainly taught by pastors who had spent many years in exile, working on farms, in factories and/or mines. Very few of them were scholars, but they had a deep passion to train the young emerging Christian leaders how to run the church well. Most of them had studied in seminaries during the period of missionary involvement when theology rooted in western thinking was taught. Thus much of what was being taught was saturated with western theological thinking.

Now the church in China stands at a crossroads. Some Christian leaders want to indigenize or bring about Sinicizing their present theology. As long as it is done within the framework of biblical truths, churches will not suffer. However, if it is moving away from it, then alarm bells are ringing.

I was glad to read an essay by one of the seminary professors in which he stated, "The significance of theological construction is first of all to guarantee that in the 21st century Chinese Christians' faith will be understood by the Chinese people, to guarantee that the Chinese church continues to advance and prosper in taking up its given responsibility and duty, and to guarantee that what the church preaches is orthodox and pure faith and doctrine. Secondly, the realization of theological construction means that the Chinese churches' reputation and prestige in the church ecumenical will finally be established. Thirdly, it means that no heresy or heterodox preaching will find any way to mislead the millions of Chinese Christians."

Yan Xiyu has this to say, "Theological reflection helps purify our Christian faith. Our faith is always guided by theological thinking; faith without theological guidance does not exist. Because of a long absence of conscious theological reflection in the Chinese church, the purity of Christian faith is subject today to the attacks from all sides. Country villages are awash with superstition, which has seriously overflowed into the churches. In the cities there are secular influences, such as the pursuit of money. How Christianity is to maintain the purity of its faith in the midst of this complex society is one of the tasks of theological construction."

The late Bishop Ting exhorted, "Theological construction is a safeguard to basic Christian faith, and it in no way attacks or changes it. Through theological construction, our faith will gain a fairer and more reasonable exposition, thereby enabling believers to have a better and more confidant understanding of their basic faith and enabling friends outside the church to be more receptive for the gospel message the church has for people."

Many of today's Chinese Christian leaders appreciate the vast amount of work my parents from a faraway country have done in their homeland.

Yes, they and countless other missionaries sowed the seed but, praise God, our Chinese brothers and sisters, who faithfully followed in their footsteps, now can reap the harvest. Both groups God used to bring about the body of Christ. But the thrilling aspect is the fact that the Chinese Christian leaders, due to the principles of self-government, self-support and self-propagation, which they embraced with full force, and under the guidance of the Holy Spirit, are now the ones who are responsible for the phenomenal church growth.

On the other hand, we have to take criticisms voiced by our Chinese friends seriously, such as expressed by a professor in one of China's theological seminaries. He writes, "The masses of church people seem to have an extremely shallow view of Christianity and thus are susceptible to cults and false teachings. What a number of Chinese scholars lament is that the Chinese church at the crucial junctures of history, at times of devastation for the nation and the people, have never of their own initiative played the just and moral role they should have taken. Western missionary evangelism in China was marked by exhorting Chinese people to abandon the Chinese cultural tradition and thus the Chinese church, which has been deeply influenced by Western missionary preaching and devotional writing, has never really reflected theologically on its own ideas of evangelism."

This, of course, in its totality, is not quite accurate. Both western and Chinese writers, teachers, scholars and missionaries have left a deep imprint on the lives of church people across China. However, we have to acknowledge the deep hurt some of our Chinese counterparts feel, as they try to evaluate the history of their own people.

One important matter must be addressed that seems to be missing in the curriculum of China's theological education. Western observers ask whether the Chinese church of today, with its absolute focus to reaching their own people, has also a vision or a strategy to fulfill Christ's mandate for world evangelization. Is this being taught? At a symposium sponsored by China Partner in conjunction with the China Christian Council, this question was put forward but not adequately answered. We all know that the Great Commission has been given to the church universal and thus no church, wherever it exists, is exempt.

In the beginning of the 21st Century, God permits us to see what our forefathers—especially those who served as missionaries in China—were not privileged to see. God is doing a mighty work of grace in the most populous country of the world. Whereas before, Christianity was seen as an alien religion that tried to enter China on the coattails of enterprising western nations, now it is accepted as a moral driving force. But what are some of the areas in which we as westerners can get involved in a meaningful way, without infringing on their rights to the Three-Self Principles? We can contribute to theological education from an evangelical perspective; we can lecture on various theological trends today; we are interested to provide funding for scholarly works; and we are interested to promote the exchange of professors of theology, just to mention a few.

The German theologian and scholar Dr. Gotthard Oblau, who with his wife lived and worked in China for twelve years (in the 1980's and 90's), writes, "Many of China's non-Christian intellectuals are interested today in a modern, enlightened Christianity such as they find in the West. Countless philosophers, historians and religious scholars, who research and teach in China's state-run institutes, study Christian thinking in the hope of finding in it something to enrich China's spiritual life, and provide a moral and spiritual counterbalance to the crude and spiritless materialism, which is spreading throughout the land at this current time."

He continues, "Theologians find it highly regrettable that the same secular intellectuals, despite their spiritual interest in Christianity, hardly find any access to the Protestant Chinese church, which due to its style and appearance does not appeal to them."

The theological training needs are great in the country, and in city churches, seminaries and Bible centers, but there is hope! God is on the move. He is using His people in China as light posts across the entire nation. Theological education is playing and will continue to play a vital role in equipping emerging young Christian leaders for the enormous task to reach out to the yet unreached one billion plus Chinese. We in Europe, Africa, North and South America, Australia, New Zealand and the Pacific, can learn much from what is transpiring in China these days.

CHAPTER 10

The lost Prayer Meeting

Here now one of the most intriguing and stimulating accounts of a prayer meeting, which God used to bring evangelism back into the forefront of Christian ministries. This also paved the way for Billy Graham's amazing life-long evangelistic career. In a vivid way, author Sherwood E. Wirt writes about The Lost Prayer Meeting.

At a time, when prayer is a lost art, and where the vast majority of Christians do not take time for private or family devotions, it is good to be reminded of instances, when prayer was taken seriously. As a result, God did mighty things. Here the story how Billy Graham was catapulted into evangelism that encompassed the entire world. More than 200 million people heard him preach in person and countless millions more were touched by his ministry through radio, television and literature. For decades he was listed as one of ten most admired persons.

All this started with a prayer meeting that we now know as *The Lost Prayer Meeting*. Here it is:

The lost Prayer Meeting
It was 3 o'clock in the morning on Wednesday, July 13, 1949. Between forty and fifty young men were gathered in the Rainbow

Room of the Westminster Hotel in Winona Lake, Indiana. They had been there for five hours – praying.

The occasion was the fifth annual convention of Youth for Christ. The newly elected president of the organization, Robert A. Cook, had sounded the keynote by telling the young rally directors from all over the United States and Canada, "The price of leadership is prayer." Evangelist Armin Gesswein of southern California, who had been invited to conduct the prayer sessions, had added, "If you are going to have prayer, it has to be frontal, not peripheral."

That was how an all-night prayer meeting happened to be called in the midst of a busy weeklong convention. The men had been alternating prayers with praise, verses of Scripture, and requests for more prayer. At midnight, Cook had challenged the group: "Who is dry? Who feels out of the will of God? Who senses that his work is fruitless?" When someone expressed a need, a brother would join him and they would move to a quiet corner for prayer.

Now it was 3 a.m., and things were beginning to warm up. Hearts were poured out before God. The tide was running high. Gesswein stood to his feet. "You know," he said, "our brother Billy Graham is coming out to Los Angeles for a Crusade this fall. Why don't we just gather around this man, lay our hands on him, and really pray for him? Let's ask God for a fresh touch to anoint him for this work."

At that time, Billy Graham was vice president of Youth for Christ. He got up from his seat, walked to the front and knelt on the oak floor. A dozen men joined him, including Gesswein and another Californian, Roy McKeown. Hands were laid gently on him who was the subject of the prayer burden, and the intercession began.

When it was over and the men were still kneeling, Billy Graham opened his Bible to Joel 3:13 and read aloud the words, "Put ye in the sickle, for the harvest is ripe: come, get you down: for the press is full, the vats overflow." Then he said, "Fellows, I'm taking that verse with me to the West Coast. I believe if we will put in the sickle, we shall reap an unprecedented harvest of souls for Christ."

Prayer went on in the Rainbow Room for another hour before the men retired. Two months later, at the corner of Washington Boulevard and Hill Street, Los Angeles, the tent Crusade began, sponsored by Christian pastors and laymen who had banded together as "Christ for Greater Los Angeles."

This is not the place to tell the story of the Crusade, of its extension to an unparalleled eight weeks, of the dramatic conversions that occurred, of the crowds that began to flock to the great tent, of the sudden nationwide interest that sprang up following a feature story in the Los Angeles *Examiner*, or of the emergence of Billy Graham's ministry as a religious phenomenon of the 20th century. Hundreds of thousands of words have been written about the events of those exciting days.

Curiously, none of the published accounts seem to have mentioned the spiritual preparation that took place at Winona Lake. Other prayer meetings related to the Crusade have been well documented: the student revival at Bethel College [now Bethel University], St. Paul, Minnesota, late in 1948; an intensive prayer meeting at Northwestern Schools [now Northwestern College], Minneapolis, in May, 1949, during the visiting ministry of J. Edwin Orr (the President of Northwestern was Billy Graham); the revival prayer conference at Pacific Palisades, California, in July, with Armin Gesswein and several hundred ministers, evangelists, missionaries and their wives; and the September college briefing conference at Forest Home, California, at which Mr. Graham was the morning speaker to some five hundred students.

All of these played a role in the spiritual groundwork for Los Angeles; and yet none of them seemed to "explain" the mid-century explosion that occurred that fall. Spiritual events always cast their shadows before them in the form of prayer. That is why I have chosen to describe what happened at Winona Lake as "the lost prayer meeting." In a way, it tells us as much about the operation of the Holy

Spirit as does the arduous and faithful preparation that went into the citywide Crusade.

Several of the men who were present in the Rainbow Room at Winona Lake have made the final transition from prayer to praise: they are forever with the Lord. Others have moved into positions of leadership in the church. None of those living have forgotten the occasion. And for us, who are members of the next generation: Is it now time to again focus on prayer at a time, when the United States under its leadership is knowingly and deliberately rejecting biblical values and truths!

CHAPTER 11

Importance of Scriptural Intake

It was in Shanghai, where I first learned how to have an intimate relationship with God. I had found this wonderful liaison by accepting Jesus as my Savior. How? When first confronted by a missionary with the question, whether I knew what it meant to be a follower of Jesus, I had to demur. I really did not know, but the question triggered in me the desire to find out. I started to search, and when I found out, it was for me a revelation of enormous consequence! It not only changed my outlook on life in general, but it radically changed my life—and that totally. It was a new beginning of a quest that now has gone on for more than seventy years. And I am still learning!

How did I start out to learn?

There is an organization that apparently very few Christians today know about. The Navigators, a Christian association, was established by Dawson Trotman (1906-1956), who in his high school years was a class valedictorian, student body president, chairman of the student council, and captain of the basketball team, but then drifted away. He started to gamble and drink, and when a policeman found him drunk one night and not able to find his car, he encouraged him to change his life style. This jolted him around. Memorizing some Bible verses clarifying salvation, he realized that he needed a savior who could forgive his sins. Only then he made a commitment to follow Christ. He was a changed person.

This man made a profound impression on me when I was struggling as a teenager. I had been raised in a godly home, went to a quality school, attended a dynamic church, but I needed guidance for my spiritual life. Going to church just didn't cut it. I wanted more. I wanted to grow spiritually.

Then I met Dawson Trotman. Speaking to our small, but lively Ambassador for Christ youth group, he challenged us to get into the Scriptures, which means to find out what the Bible is all about and above all, what it teaches. To explain, he drew a hand with its five outstretched fingers on the blackboard.

The little finger stands for Hearing the Word of God. That is what most Christians do. They go to church, some more often than others, and that is the place where they hear what the Bible teaches. However, there are dangers lurking, because not all pastors and preachers expound the unadulterated truth. But the fact is, that hearing the Word of God is a good thing, and it should be encouraged in spite of the risks involved.

The ring finger stands for Reading the Word of God. Less Christians have the habit of doing just that. I wager to say, that most of the believers have not developed the habit of taking some time each day to read the Bible. No doubt, all Christians have a Bible in their homes, but how many read them? I have seen them as ornaments displayed in noticeable spots of a home or on book shelves. Some even have several versions! But they are not being read habitually. In order to grow spiritually as a Christian, it is a must to read the Bible.

The middle finger stands for Studying the Word of God. This takes a huge amount of effort and time to do. I remember as a new believer, I filled note books upon note books of thoughts that I gathered as I studied the Bible. It was not easy and it took real discipline. However, it was worth it.

The fore finger or index finger stands for Memorizing the Word of

God. Herein most of the believers fail. How many of your friends do you know who are memorizing Bible verses? Some of us remember the Sunday school days, when we were challenged to memorize. In fact we were pitched one against another in congenial competition. And it was fun. But those days are gone, and most of us have disregarded this important tool for spiritual growth.

Finally, the thumb stands for Meditating on the Word of God. We can and should utilize this technique for all of the above mentioned tools: meditate on what you just heard, read, studied and memorized. This will undoubtedly help you to become a strong Christian, rightly dividing the Word of truth (1.Timothy 4.15).

While writing this book, I was challenged again personally to pick up where I may have slacked off as I am getting older. Until death there is still room to grow—in fact in a lot of areas! All believers are called to fight on in their daily lives. Paul put it succinctly this way, "…but this one thing I do, forgetting those things that are behind, and reaching forth unto those things that are before, I press toward the mark for the prize of the high calling of God in Christ Jesus (Philippians 3.13,14).

CHAPTER 12

The small woman

Port Sudan, the port city on the eastern side of the African coast and only one-hundred miles across from Jiddah in Saudi Arabia, was chosen by the captain of our ship ss. Rena, to take some fuel aboard. We were on a long journey from China to Europe. He originally had been scheduled to dock his vessel in Aden, five-hundred miles further south, but at all the ports previously visited, he had left without paying the compulsory harbor fees. So now he showed up in ports where no one expected him. He was a crook. And I was one of the passengers of his dreadful ship!

Thank God, we were allowed to go on land. What a relief! After having been aboard this wretched boat for many weeks, we wanted to see something different. We looked for excitement. This 2,000 ton ship had previously plowed the English Channel between Dover and Calais as a ferry. It had nothing to offer in entertainment: No games, no swimming pool, no library, no recreational activities—absolutely nothing! As I described this episode in my former book *Hitler, Mao, & Jesus,* it was a monotonous and dreary time onboard. The English Admiralty used to say, "Join the navy and see the world." But the reality was different, and that's why the British sailors added to it the catchphrase or jingle, "What did we see? We saw the sea." And that's exactly what we saw! We saw the sea.

But we did have some wonderful fellowship with passengers, who were Christian missionaries. Every day we met for devotions to study the Bible. These periods sometimes extended into hours, because there was so much to share. One lady especially stood out. She hailed from England. Gladys Aylward (1902-1970) was born to lowly parents in London. For several years she worked as a parlor-maid and was miraculously converted to Christ. Later, in one of the revival meetings held in her area, she felt called to become a missionary. China became the focus of her attention and then of her heart, and she never wavered, even when seasoned Christian leaders tried to discourage her. "You are not too smart," they said, "you will never be able to learn one of the most difficult language in the world—Chinese."

Even the well-seasoned and experienced leaders at the London headquarters of the China Inland Mission at Newton Green tried to discourage her, when she failed to live up to the standards they had set for missionary candidates. She had tried hard but had failed in their eyes. So she returned to be a parlor-maid, discouraged but not dejected nor disheartened. Her dream to go to China never diminished. She simply pressed on.

Day after day she worked and saved every penny she could get hold of. She had saved three Pounds Sterling when she finally made contact with a travel agency. The travel agent advised, it would be cheaper to travel by train through Russia than by ship via the Indian Ocean. But to take the land route would be dangerous and ill advised, because a severe military conflict was raging between Russia and China at the eastern end of the railroad in Siberia. In the book *The Small Woman*, we read:

> "I couldn't really care about a silly war," she had told
> the agent. "It's the cheapest way, isn't it? That's what
> I want. Now, if you'll book me a passage, you can

have these three pounds on account and I'll pay you as much as I can every week."

Exactly what she thought she would be able to do when she arrived in China without a penny in her pocket, and not understanding a word of the language, she hardly knew herself. She was determined, nevertheless, that even if she could not pass through the scholastic eye of the China Inland Mission needle, she could at least equip herself as an evangelist and know the Bible intimately. "I must learn to preach, she said to herself. "I must learn to talk to the people."

So, besides working as a parlor-maid, in every moment of spare time she stood on a soup box at the well-known Hyde Park, learning how to preach. She also read profusely any book on China or stories of missionaries. Gladys was a determined, strong-minded and a gritty woman.

Finally, as a twenty-six year old she left England for good. What an amazing trip by the Trans-Siberian Railroad across Holland, Germany, Poland, the Soviet Union (USSR), Japan and finally China! She only made one mistake, and that was a very big one. In the middle of Siberia, when she should have transferred to another train in the city of Chita, she stayed on, and with her a horde of Russian soldiers who were on the way to a military base some fifty miles further on. When all of them disembarked, she was told that this was the end of the route. Now she was stuck!

With no trains returning, she grabbed her two suitcases and had to trek back along the railroad tracks. It took her two days. She would never forget that solemn night, sleeping in a forlorn forest covered with snow, as the violent winter gusts would bite into her skin, and howling wolves were frightening her to death.

Back in Chita she found the right train and finally arrived in

Vladivostok, then traveling on by ship to Japan and from there to Tientsin, todays Tianjin, in China. But it took her another four weeks to reach her final destination Yangchen, near Tsechow, in the province of Shanxi (North China region, south-west of Beijing), one of the earliest cultural and political provinces of China.

Here she started her amazing ministry. We sat spellbound as she took us in our minds back to China from where we had just come. I had lived a calm and comfortable life in Shanghai and had no idea what missionaries had to endure in other areas. Also my parents, who had labored in the province of Jiangxi had nothing to compare to her hardships. Yes, they had to flee from marauding communist troops. They had to endure being interned by the Nationalist authorities during the Second World War. They were cut off from their three children for more than five years. But nothing like Gladys Aylward encountered!

As a young Christian and as a teenager, I was eager to learn from faithful and experienced men or women of God how to shape the future of my life. Gladys was someone I could look up to and admire. At that time she was not famous. She was not interested in becoming a rich person or a political celebrity. She was a simple, down-to-earth and unpretentious person, and someone I could venerate. This is how Alan Burgess, the author of *The Small Woman,* put it:

> Gladys Aylward is shy, and very modest. She carries these things in her heart; she rarely speaks of them. A little parlor-maid from London traveled alone across Siberia, because of a single letter from a woman she had never met….A young girl lived alone for years in a remote mountain city, speaking a strange language, wearing native clothes, becoming friend and counselor to a people so foreign in thought and culture that at first their every custom must have seemed alien. A single-minded and determined girl conversed for

hours with a learned Mandarin as he propounded the intricate subtleties of his philosophy. Yet, armed only with her own forthright experience and inspired intuitions, she converted him finally to Christianity. A woman, tireless and fearless, traveled alone, month after month, through the dangerous mountain regions of Shansi, on errands of mercy, and errands of war.

This woman was Gladys Aylward, Ai-weh-deh, the Virtuous One. They will not forget her in Shansi. And those who have known her since will not forget her either. For Gladys Aylward is one of the remarkable women of our generation, possessing an inner exaltation, and an abiding tenacity of purpose, that can make anything possible. Even a trip across the wild and pitiless mountains of China, without money, without food, and with a hundred children.

For us teenagers, those stories hit home. Those were actual experiences of what followers of Jesus had to endure, once having committed themselves to missionary endeavor in a distant and alien country. To me, borne in China, and having lived a comfortable and interesting life in cosmopolitan Shanghai, it was a unique education. It all sounded so exciting.

Another of her experience showed what kind of a courageous woman she was. James Kiefer elaborated on this further:

During her second year in Yangchen, Gladys was summoned by the Mandarin. A riot had broken out in the men's prison. She arrived and found that the convicts were rampaging in the prison courtyard, and several of them had been killed. The soldiers were afraid to intervene. The warden of the prison said to Gladys, "Go into the yard and stop the rioting." She said, "How can I do that?" The warden of the prison said, "You have been preaching that those who trust in Christ have nothing to fear." So she walked into the courtyard and shouted: "Quiet! I cannot hear when everyone is shouting at once. Choose one or two spokesmen, and let me talk with them." The men quieted down and chose a spokesman. Gladys talked with him, and then came out and told the warden:" You have these men cooped up in crowded conditions with absolutely nothing to do. No wonder they are so edgy that a small dispute sets off a riot. You must give them work. Also, I am told that you do not supply food for them, so that they have only what their relatives send them. No wonder they fight over food. We will set up looms so that they can weave cloth and earn enough money to buy their own food." This was done. There was no money for sweeping reforms, but a few friends of the warden donated old looms, and a grindstone so that the men could work grinding grain.

As I said above, I along with the other teenagers from Shanghai sat spellbound listening to this brave and daring lady as we all headed for Europe. When we finally had to say good-bye to her in Marseilles, France, on April 15, 1949, I was determined to keep in touch with her. We corresponded for several years, when finally on January 3, 1970 she passed on to glory in Taiwan. To her last breath she served her Lord. One of her famous retort to a concerned General Ley, who had feared for her life and warned her to retreat to safer grounds was, "Christians never retreat!"

Gladys Aylward lived to the fullest and died as a hero. She never retreated.

CHAPTER 13

Wang Mingdao and Henry

Wang Mingdao was a Chinese Christian who stood up for his faith when heavily attacked. During the Cultural Revolution in China (1966-76), when all religious people were persecuted, including Buddhists, Taoists, Muslim and Christians, he was thrown into prison. He was forced to write down his confession about the life he had lived. This was the way the Communists tried to control the minds of its citizens. When those confessions were inadequate in the minds of the tormentors, they had to be rewritten. And that again and again to fully satisfy the interrogators. Some went insane after a while, others even committed suicide when they no longer could bear such treatment. Others broke and submitted to the demands of the rulers.

Wang Mingdao broke. With this he was released from prison.

Walking the streets of Beijing again as a free man, he reflected on what had transpired. He shuddered, because he suddenly realized what he had done, and with it how low he had sunk in respectability and decency! While battling this out in his mind, he could no longer live with this impiety. In distress and agony he cried out, "I am Peter, I am Peter, and have denied my Lord." When this had really sunk in, and when he could no longer live with what he had done, he went back to the authorities and recanted what he had written down. As a consequence he was thrown back into prison. He was incarcerated for "twenty-three years minus two months," as he later told me. Eventually he was released and exonerated.

But what caused Wang Mingdao to come successfully through such an ordeal and thereby becoming an ardent follower of Jesus Christ? What was his secret? Well, he based his conviction on the cross that Jesus had to endure. When Christ had to bear such a burden for mankind, and thus for him, Wang Mingdao felt to embrace the cross as well—his cross being thrown into prison. Therefore, let us take a closer look at what the Bible teaches about the centrality of the cross.

The Old and New Testament are repeatedly focusing on this all-important truth. Here are just a few sections: (Isaiah 53.3-12; Matthewv20.19, 27.31-44; 1. Corinthians 1.13; Galatians 2.19; Hebrews 12.2).

Of course there have been other noteworthy religious founders or originators, such as Confucius (551-479 BC), Buddha (563-483 BC), Zoroaster (dates unknown), Krishna (3228-3102 BC), Mohammed (571-632 BC), Joseph Smith (1805-44 AD) and others. To know Confucius, you point to his wise teachings. To know Buddha, you point to his temples. To know Zoroaster, you point to Persian philosophy. To know Krishna, you point to the Godhead of Hindu deities. To know Mohammed, you point to the Koran. To know Joseph Smith, you point to the impressive Mormon Temple.

However to know Jesus, you point to the cross, and not to his "sermon on the mount," nor to great cathedrals. No, you point to the cross—the expression of His love.

Nevertheless, we can get so used to the significance of our faith that we tend to often forget and ignore the centrality of the cross. That's why we have to look at this more closely. Interestingly there is a negative and a positive side to the cross. The negative aspect includes the following:

- The ugliness of Christ hanging on the cross, spittle mixed with blood covering his body. People turned away from this terrible spectacle—this was the true picture of Jesus on the cross.
- Great artists throughout centuries tried to patch up this ugly side—some painters painted the softer side of the cross, and some musicians composed splendid pieces minimizing the importance of the cross.
- But Jesus did not die in a gorgeous cathedral between two chandeliers—two gangsters were on either side.
- Even His disciples could not bear the sight—they ran away.
- The Roman soldiers almost had a nervous breakdown when they were forced to crucify him—one of them even said, "Truly, this was the Son of God."
- Today some try to remove the ugly cross from the epicenter to a place hidden in the background.
- But there is also the positive side of the cross, which clarifies the central theme of the gospel.
- We are not saved through Christ's miracles, nor His sinless life, not even through His resurrection—it was done through His death on the cross.
- Hegel: "The cross is the very axis of human experience."
- Therefore we all have to play part in another chapter—the chapter of "blessing."
- When we look into the face of Jesus, we look into our own face.
- He hangs on the cross for you and me.

This was portrayed so well by Rembrandt in his painting *"Night watch"*, displayed in Amsterdam. It is a gorgeous yet somber painting of the crucifixion. You see groups of people and as you look closer, you will see their attitudes written on the faces—some look mockingly, fearfully, sadly, curiously, gratefully, and others with brutality. On the low right hand corner of the painting you can make out the self-portrait of Rembrandt.

If I give Jesus my lostness—He gives security. If I give Jesus my disaster—He returns order into victory. If I give Jesus my life—He exchanges eternal death with everlasting life through His death on the cross. What do I mean? What is so important about the cross? Let me show it with an illustration.

An Italian village experienced the Bubonic plague—known as the Black Death. The people first turned to God and when it got worse, they turned against Him. They got drunk—an orgy of desperation took place; many people died, left lying in the streets.

Then there was a strange sound coming up the mountain—monks carrying a big cross and chanting, "Lord, have mercy on us." People of the village mock them, "There is no God." They move to and then finally into the wide-open village church. People crowd in with them.

*A young lad jumps onto the altar and shouts, "God is dead, let's get drunk and be merry." Then one of the monks goes to the pulpit and softly speaks about Jesus and His crucifixion. He tells them how the people **then** had mocked Him. What did Jesus say in response? Did He declare, "Should I die for those rotten people?" No! Did He get down from the cross to disappear into heaven? No!*

The monk continued, "If He would have done that, there would be no salvation, no hope, and no redemption for any of us."

When the young man recognized the truth of this, he wildly stretched out his hand, and in agony he shouts to the monk, "Put the Savior back onto the cross!"

You see, the young man realized that without the cross there is no hope. If Jesus were removed from the cross, there is death. Death for you and me.

What were some of the experiences missionaries to China had before Mao's rule started in the year 1949? Their message of the cross was new to the Chinese and was rejected. They were called foreign devils. Christianity along with imperialism was a huge stumbling block to the Chinese, and they fought to bring about the decline and finally the collapse of the British Empire and with it the termination of foreign powers' domination in general. The national pride of the Chinese, due to her 6.000 year culture, made it imperative for them to get rid of the over-lording of all foreigners. And out of this, however, Christian men like Wang Mingdao came to the fore, and he along with others developed to sinicize the church in China.

Another one was Henry in the northern city of Baoding. He was not famous as Wang Mingdao, but he experienced God's mighty work as well, while going through a period of suffering and misery, which ultimately resulted in a glorious outcome.

I met Henry in Baoding after his release from imprisonment. Born in Hawaii on December 16, 1926, he returned to his homeland in 1932 along with his Chinese parents. He was a quiet, shy, but a dedicated young man when he joined our group, the Ambassadors for Christ in Shanghai. Desiring to lift his people out of disease and poverty, he studied medicine. As a young surgeon he worked at the Eastern Shanghai Hospital, but then the political situation changed, and he became a victim of communistic ideology.

Having been brought up in a forward-looking family, Henry was not content with the belligerent propaganda the new regime offered. The leaders talked about building a new society, but instead they enslaved the people by putting their minds in chains. Wanting to be free, Henry listened on the radio to the Voice of America and the BBC, which the government had forbidden. Despite the risk, he yearned for news of events from the rest of the world. One day law enforcement agents rushed into his home, demanding, "Turn off that radio! You are under arrest."

One of his friends had betrayed him.

"Why do you go against the law? You are a spy!" his interrogators accused him. "You know it is prohibited to listen to your enemies."

"I am not a spy."

"But you are engaged in activities that are harmful to our country. Foreign radio broadcasts will defile your mind."

"How can that be?" Henry insisted. "My parents lived in Hawaii, where I was born, but chose to return to the land they loved. They taught me to love my country and build up the nation. What is wrong about finding out how people live in other countries? Furthermore, I am a Christian and only want to do what is honorable. So was Sun Yat-sen, whom you admire. Look at his statue in Nanjing and at the pompous mausoleum on the hill."

"We despise Christianity! Marx taught that religion is the opiate of the people. So did Lenin," they insisted.

Being a Christian and listening to foreign radio broadcasts landed him first in prison and then in a labor camp in the province of Anhui. Those were dreadful years. Among hundreds of others, he was forced to do hard labor. He slept body to body in shacks. "In the winter some of my friends froze to death, and in the summer the heat sapped us of all strength," he told me.

Released from imprisonment in 1980, Henry was banished to Baoding, a city south-west of Beijing. He was forced to work as an interpreter in one of the many state industrial unit. The sun beat down heavily as I disembarked at the run-down railroad station. Baoding is certainly not a tourist spot. But I had come to Baoding to meet him. Masses of people flooded the square facing the railroad station.

Amazing crowds, but 1.3 billion inhabitants crowd its cities, towns and villages.

Where is Henry?

A large straw hat covered his head as he slowly approached me. He looked so old. Years of hard labor had worn down his body, giving him a frail appearance. His delicate fingers, which used to handle surgical instruments and scalpels, now looked like stumps on his hands. Henry's eyes reflected sadness and fear. "Chinese 'CIA agents' are everywhere," he cautioned. "I don't trust anyone. I love China with its beautiful landmarks, unique architecture, unparalleled skill, cloisonné, and curiosities. But I cannot forget the pain the system had inflicted upon me. True, it has improved lately, but they cannot erase what is engraved in my memory."

His suffering had made Henry a lonely, wounded man. After all of those horrendous experiences throughout the prime of his life, he now lived in a place totally removed from his loved ones. His parents had died during the Cultural Revolution. His close friends lived overseas. No family, no wife, no Christian fellowship, no Bible, no church to attend. He was all alone and broken in spirit. A wasted life like countless others in an oppressed land!

Henry was just one of the persecuted Christians I met on my travels in China. He was one of many heroes in that land. To understand what I mean, you have to read the chilling passage in Hebrews 11.

CHAPTER 14

Bridging the Gulf between Christians in China

The divisions of the body of Christ in China caused by Satan challenged me to always identify with the entire and true body of Christ, and then to serve those belonging to it. Since 1981, when I began to visit China on a regular basis, I endeavored to understand the political situation, to get the right perspective, and to see the total picture of the all-inclusive body of Christ.

On my first trip to China, I stopped in Hong Kong and met with so-called China specialists and China watchers. I took their advice seriously to be on guard against the "wolves in sheep's clothing", as they put it. They warned me against contacting Christians of the "Three-Self-Patriotic-Movement" (TSPM), but rather to meet with leaders of house churches. As mentioned, I took this advice seriously, and planned my trip accordingly. In the interior of China, I had difficulty finding house churches. When I finally did so in a large city, I managed to meet with the leader of one house church. I was very impressed with his dedication and the Christians associated with him. One of those believers led me to a newly opened registered church and left me there. He refused to attend the church service with me, because he did not want to worship God with those believers. This startled me! I, on the other hand, was overwhelmed by the number of believers gathered together and by the unanimity and dedication of the Christians in that church. After this experience, I vowed not to seek one above the other group of believers, but rather seek fellowship with all of those who belong to the true body of Christ. It no longer mattered to me whether believers belonged to registered churches, or non-registered churches known as house churches. Then I became painfully aware of how deep the gulf was between those two groups, and it was difficult at first to understand the reasons for such a division. The more I tried to discover the reasons, the stronger my desire grew to maintain fellowship with all believers of the body of Christ, no matter where they worshipped. Building bridges became my watchword, because filling trenches was almost impossible to achieve. As time went by, the longing grew ever deeper to fellowship with all of the believers in China, and to steer away from the counsel of those overseas Christians who had encouraged me to see and fellowship only with one group—their group. Thereby, I believed I would have genuine opportunity to help build the kingdom of God on earth.

However, then I got into a dilemma. In order to work with non-registered churches, I was told I would have to work in secrecy. This was contrary to my convictions. I wish to avoid judging those who have chosen to take that route. It would take too long to explain why I personally had problems with their logic. Before going into China on my first trip, I had a motto, which has remained with me on all subsequent trips, "Lord, give me courage to do the unusual, and the sensitivity to know when to stop." So far, I have made close to 100 trips into China.

From the beginning, there was the desire to do everything openly, honestly, and legally. This led to work with the registered church, the churches of the China Christian Council (CCC). And what a blessing it became! However, I also told their leaders that I wanted to maintain further contact with leaders of non-registered churches since they also belong to the body of Christ, and that I would do nothing to hinder the development of the church in China.

The fact remains that a gulf had been fixed between those two groups. I had to come to terms with that fact.

What caused this gulf? And how could this gulf be bridged? Should we from other parts of the world help our Chinese brothers and sisters in bridging this gulf? Or would this cause religious and political authorities in China to misinterpret this as interference from outside? I did not think so, but, if done, it had to be done with understanding and spiritual sensitivity. Therefore, let me point out the historical and political background of the problem facing us today.

The Historical Background

Christianity in China was an alien religion because it was seen as foreign. My parents, who had been missionaries in China with the China Inland Mission, were called "foreign devils." What was the reason for the Chinese to see it that way?

China always has been a proud and patriotic nation. It is a highly cultured country with a four thousand-year history. During the last two hundred years, China had to accept numerous humiliations forced upon her by foreign governments. Events like the opium war, the arrow war, and the "unequal treaties" caused China to be bitter towards foreigners. In the wake of foreign military and economic advances into China, mission organizations were able to use such advantage to spread the gospel. This caused the Chinese to resist even the work of well-meaning missionaries. Most of the early missionaries did not at first recognize the reason behind such Chinese hostility. They had come in obedience to the Lord, who had said, "Go, and make disciples of all nations." Let me repeat again, and this should never be forgotten that missionaries came to China with a deep conviction of God's mandate and call. They had been motivated by the love of Jesus to serve in China. Even though the Communist government in the past tried for decades to degrade the work of missionaries, today many acknowledge once more the true and loving motives of most missionaries. Especially the younger generation of today and the young leaders of the church understand this.

Corruption caused by warlords and later on by the Nationalists, drove many Chinese into the arms of the Communists during the twenties and thirties of the 20th Century. Did Communism not promise equality for all Chinese, patriotism for their country, and the removal of all injustice? What noble goals! Even Christians were brought under the spell of this new ideology. Especially Christians with liberal theology were susceptible to these new ideas. They wanted to be part of the greater movement of those who dreamed of a new, stronger, and more glorious China!

The Political Development After 1949

"China finally stood up," announced Mao Zedong on October 1, 1949 overlooking the Tian-an-men Square. China again would belong entirely to the Chinese. China again would determine how she would live. All foreigners were asked to leave the country. Before doing so, all foreign companies and mission organizations had to undergo strict investigations and inspections by the new rulers. Everyone had to provide evidence or proof that they had not mistreated the Chinese during their stay in China, and only then were they allowed leaving the country. My parents were finally let go in 1950.

To oversee matters of the Protestant church in China, the government established the institution "Three-Self-Patriotic-Movement" (TSPM). This was done in the early fifties. Everything and everybody in China had to submit to the will of the Party. Consequently, all Christian churches were obliged to submit to this movement. Many of them did, others did not. Bible-believing and evangelical Christians, especially those from independent (non-denominational or non-confessional) churches, particularly those that had been started by Chinese, were reluctant to join the new and quasi-political structure. A number of those church leaders, preachers, pastors and evangelists were arrested and sentenced to imprisonment.

The TSPM, established by the Party, was subject to its political interpretation. Government policies could then be imposed upon the churches.

What is the meaning of Three-Self?

Self-Supporting—to be financially independent and forbidden to accept foreign support.

Self-Propagating—to proclaim the gospel only through the Chinese themselves and not from abroad.

Self-Governing—to independently lead and care for the church in China without depending upon foreign involvement.

According to the constitution of 1954, the People's Republic of China assured every citizen "liberty and religious freedom," as spelled out in Article 88. The reality, however, proved to be different. The oppression against Christians continued.

The worst persecution of the Communist era took place during the Cultural Revolution (1966-76). All churches were closed, the Bible was forbidden, and Christians could only meet secretly in small groups.

Throughout mission history in China, suffering was a key element in church life. On different occasions, Christianity became extinct. For example, the Nestorians were muted in the ninth century, and in the fourteenth century, the Franciscans experienced the same fate. After the Communists took power in 1949 (in China this is referred to as "liberation"), and particularly during the Cultural Revolution, continuous persecution was severe, which included imprisonment, exile, labor camps, and sometimes death. This period of suffering and the succeeding resurrection of the Chinese church can be seen in five different periods. However, it must be stated that not only Christians suffered, but followers of other religions did as well. Here, however, we want to focus on the plight of Christians.

1. The Body of Christ during Oppression (1949-58)

After "liberation", the government tried to completely subjugate the churches under state rule. In the early years of Communist rule, their goal was to prevent all contact between Christians in China and their foreign "mother churches." Foreign missionaries were expelled and those who tried to remain in the country were charged during "struggle meetings" and often sentenced. At times, Chinese Christians were executed. Many institutions operated by Christians, such as mission schools, hospitals, orphanages, schools for the blind, and church buildings were closed or taken over by the party or municipal governments.

2. The Body of Christ during Times of Hardship (1958-66)

During this period, the Communist government eased up on its persecution of the church. Christians were allowed to practice their faith with more freedom. However, the Party increased its pressure against churches to rid themselves totally of all foreign influences. Their desire was to purify the church from any remaining foreign influence and "capitalistic imperialism." During this period the split between believers and the churches reached its peak—one group led by the TSPM, and the other by leaders of non-registered churches. The latter were seen as illegal and thus persecuted.

3. The Body of Christ Threatened by Extinction (1966-76)

During this decade, also called "the lost decade," the Cultural Revolution brought turmoil to the entire country during which time hundreds of thousands of people died (possibly even millions), and a number of those victims were Christians. All Christians were forced underground, and only thus were they able to survive. Only within the confines of their immediate family were Christians able to live out their faith.

4. The Period of Slow Awakening of the Body of Christ (1976-79)

After Chou En-lai and Mao Zedong had died in 1976, some of the government policies were changed. Government leaders realized how dependent they were upon the expertise and investments of industrialized Western powers. Furthermore, they needed to become true partners of the world's community. This, of course, alleviated the pressure on all religious communities. In 1979, the first church was opened in Ningbo (Zhejiang), then in Shanghai, Beijing, and other cities followed rapidly.

5. The Body of Christ in the New China (1979 to present)

Presently over 21 million Christians can worship freely in over 15,000 church buildings and at least 30,000 registered house churches also called meeting points. Other millions assemble in non-registered house churches. Christians who meet in churches and meeting points affiliated with the CCC can easily be counted, and its numbers can be substantiated. This is not the case with those that meet in non-registered house churches. A survey done by China Partner revealed between 38-41 million Protestant Christians

The CCC, which oversees and regulates the interests of registered churches, was established in the early eighty's and has since proven to be a binding force among churches. The Council is in close contact with foreign denominations and Christian organizations. Unfortunately, many overseas evangelical leaders are still reluctant to cooperate, fellowship, and to befriend believers within the churches of the CCC. I deeply regret the fact that the gulf between believers of the body of Christ, which initially was caused by the political development in China, has not been overcome due to attitudes among a number of some evangelicals overseas. In China itself, efforts are being made to find ways of rapprochement; overseas such efforts are not made, or very cautiously at best. In a number of regions in China, house churches have now registered with the government and thus found fellowship with the CCC. The spirit of reconciliation, extended more readily by members of the CCC, is finally bearing fruit.

Dr. Kleiner, a former missionary to Africa with the Swiss Alliance Mission, traveled to China with a China Partner teaching team, and reported, "The China Christian Council has been and still is ostracized by many evangelicals in the West. The reasons are a) because the Communist government supposedly controls the CCC and/or b) she has contact with the World Council of Churches. Some even say that leaders of CCC have learned the vocabulary of evangelical Christians in order to delude evangelical visitors from overseas. The truth, however, (so say the critics) is that they are not Christians at all, but they are only pretending. In my opinion, it is unjustified and tragic to avoid Christians within the CCC, because by doing so it affects and hurts the entire body of Christ worldwide. It deprives evangelicals of the possibility to share in the awakening and in the spiritual life that is taking place within the CCC. By doing so, it only leads and encourages members of the CCC to move to a closer contact with theologically liberal churches in the West. The general notion that leaders of the CCC are not Christians at all is very painful to them and to us as well who fellowship with those believers . . . according to my experience it is wrong to say that Christians of the CCC are spiritually cold, liberal or dead. To the contrary, we encountered dynamic spiritual life."

This is exactly what I have experienced on all my trips to China. Of course, like everything else in life, there are exceptions. However, by far most of the Christians in China, who belong to CCC churches, are Bible believing, Christ-centered, and evangelical.

What Are the Reasons for the Tensions that Exist Between the Two Groups?

We are talking about tensions that exist between church leaders of the CCC and leaders of various groups within the house church movement. Even today, many leaders of house churches refuse to fellowship with those that belong to CCC churches, and they refuse to register their churches with the authorities. In the past, registrations had to be made with the TSPM. Several years ago, this regulation changed so that house churches can register directly with municipal authorities.

A dear brother, who is an elder in one of the CCC churches in Shanghai, regrets this division. He believes there are three main reasons why house church leaders do not want to unite with the CCC:

1. In the early days (before the Cultural Revolution), some of the leaders of the TSPM collaborated with the Communist regime.

2. Leaders of house churches act rather independently and thus are responsible to no one. In order to keep their position of power within their respective groups, they continue to foster resentment against the CCC and its leadership, and thus foster enmity.

3. Christians, who years ago fled China, cannot forget the reason for having done so. Now, having the opportunity to visit their former homeland, they sow seeds of division and stir up distrust against the CCC.

There is a deep desire among leaders within house churches to live out their faith in total freedom and to spread the gospel throughout their country. On the other hand, and unfortunately so, large segments within the house church movement have distanced themselves from biblical foundations and propagate heretical teachings—some of them have become cults. This is a sore spot often mentioned by leaders of the CCC. Christian leaders in China have told me that some of the heresies are homegrown and others have been imported from overseas.

A foreign observer mentions three reasons he feels are put forth by those who refuse to register.

1. Political—rejection of Communism.

2. Historical—denunciation of non-registered churches by those who belong to the TSPM, especially in the period before the Cultural Revolution.

3. Theological—rejection of liberal theology found within sections of the TSPM; rigidity in believing that their faith (house church) alone is the correct one and therefore they rigorously refuse to work together with other churches and Christians.

In order to understand the reasons for the gulf that now exists between the two groups, and the ones that brought it about, we must explore the background that led to the split during the period of Communist rule. Christianity in China had to prove itself over a period of decades. Let me mention five different aspects:

1. Political—as mentioned earlier, China has always been a patriotic (nationalistic) country. She considered herself the center of the world. Today you can still visit a spot in Beijing, which, according to the Chinese, is seen as the "Center of the World." Did missionaries have enough sensitivity to really understand this political issue?

2. Cultural—China is the country with the oldest culture. Throughout the centuries, civilizations cultivated in China, and great teachers determined the development of the country. The best known and most esteemed of those was the sage Confucius (551-479 BC), whose teachings during the approaching millennia became the backbone of Chinese

civilization. How did the missionaries confront these well-established ethical teachings with its *Weltanschauung*?

3. Religious—religions such as Buddhism and Taoism had existed in China for a long period, and they viewed Christianity as a danger. Did missionaries have to meet head-on with proponents of these religions and study its teachings? Of course. The question is **how** did they confront those well-rooted religions?

4. Historical—different types of mission organizations worked in China. There were those that belonged to liberal organizations, and others that belonged to evangelical groups. Later Chinese Christians established their own mission organizations and often did not like to cooperate with their foreign counterparts. When the TSPM was established, it enhanced the split between the leadership of registered and non-registered churches.

5. Human—as found in countries the world over, there are differences of opinions regarding interpretation of the Bible, and the perception of Christian beliefs. Watchman Nee, for example, was exclusive in his stance and had difficulty working with foreigners. He even had problems working with Chinese Christians, who were under the jurisdiction of foreign mission boards. This resulted in unspiritual and carnal mindsets, which, of course, hindered the unity of Christians.

What then can we, as foreigners, contribute to building bridges, or better yet, help bridging the gulf?

Let me mention three areas:

1. *Avoid what could be seen as negative and interpreted as such, which easily results in negative thinking.* For example:

    a. Do not make unsubstantiated claims as to how many Christians live in China today. No one knows! Surveys show there are between 39 – 41 million.

    b. Do not criticize leading Christians, no matter what group they belong to in China.

    c. Don't make false declarations about persecuted Christians in China, like "60 million Christians in China are brutally persecuted today," as was stated in an evangelical video. Who has actually counted those 60 million? Or on the other hand, why do so many suppress the fact that there are at least 21 million Christians who freely assemble to worship God and live out their faith without fear?

    d. Don't declare that persecution of Christians is a planned policy of China's government. It is not! Everybody knows that bad news travels faster than good news, and some relish in propagating bad news. The son of a much-respected church leader in the United States told me once "it is a shame that Christians overseas have lowered themselves to the extent that they raise funds on the back of formerly persecuted Chinese Christians."

2. *Be Willing to Highlight the Positive Development of the Body of Christ in China.*

    It is important to mention the positive side of what is happening in China and by doing so encourage our fellow believers. However, I want to caution against overly highlighting and exaggerating the positive developments. But we must be fair and balanced in our reporting. The positive side needs to be reported. There are numerous advancements to rejoice in. We can be grateful for the positive improvement in China in areas of economics and culture; for the incredible resurrection of the church after the terrible period of the Cultural Revolution; for the growth of the church in China which is estimated to have a constituency of over 38 million (including members of non-registered churches); for opportunities in some parts of China to again do youth and Sunday School work; for the majority of Christians in China who are Bible-believing and evangelical; for the great interest shown in the gospel by university students and intellectuals; for over 100 million Bibles that have been printed since the Cultural Revolution; for theological seminaries and Bible schools that are operative in twenty-three cities across China where about 1,500 students are being trained for the Lord's work; for Christians in China that are actively engaged in humanitarian effort; for the improved relationship between house churches and the CCC in many areas; and for the CCC's effort to cooperate with evangelicals abroad.

One of my great concerns is that many churches lack well-trained pastors and church workers. However, there are only a few theological schools overseas, which are willing to give scholarships to theological students from China. Furthermore, it is a shame that evangelicals in a biased and unbalanced fashion often report the situation in China, and that horror stories of the past are constantly put forth.

3. *Make an effort to have fellowship with **all** believers across China.*

It is evident that evangelicals from overseas have gravitated to believers of non-registered house churches and tried to help them. This is good and should be done in the future. However, do it openly, legally, and honestly as done by a number of evangelical groups. But for the same reason, evangelicals should also be willing to fellowship with Christians of the CCC and undergird them with prayers and support. The vast majority of CCC church members—as among the non-registered Christians—are true believers who love the Lord Jesus and with whom we can have wonderful fellowship in the gospel. As for those who live as nominal Christians, friendly relationships should be maintained, so that they also may sense our desire to lift up Jesus who wants to be Lord of **all.**

Much has changed for the positive in China, and we thank God for the phenomenal church growth in that land. Even though there are remaining gulfs separating Christians from Christians, we rejoice with those that have bridged the gulf and found each other. It is my prayer that we in foreign countries help build those bridges. Let us pray with Jesus, "I have declared unto them your name, and will declare it: that the love wherewith you have loved me may be in them, and I in them" (John 17.23).

CHAPTER 15

Misconceptions about China

My response to an article published in CT

I am an avid reader of Christianity Today (CT). However, I was disturbed with your article written by Sheryl Henderson Blunt. She tried to be balanced, but left out some important issues. After the misfortune of Luis Palau's remarks and the strong criticisms he received from some Christian groups, he called me to get my reaction. I agreed with him that he should not have revealed his convictions, and I told him so. However, what he said was correct. If all of the unregistered churches would register with the government, as more and more are doing so now (and as it is being done in the United States), Christian church leaders would not be prosecuted for engaging in illegal activities. I also do not agree with some of the restrictions the Chinese government places on its citizens, but I praise God for relative freedom they now experience. The constant criticism some of the Christian groups in the West direct at the Chinese government is counterproductive. Also, for them to encourage house church leaders to continue to resist the policies of the government only enhances the hardships for those people.

It is a shame that your writer could not quote from the rebuttal given by the *China Christian Council (CCC)* to the report of the

United States Commission on International Religious Freedom. I will attach it for your perusal. Having traveled to China some 100 times since 1981, and having preached and ministered hundreds of times across China, I am surprised that false information is constantly being put forth by the media, even evangelical media. Just to mention a few examples:

1. It is not true that members of registered churches have to pay allegiance first to the government and then to Christ.

2. It is not true that sermons on the Second Coming of Christ are not allowed to be preached in registered churches (It may be conceivable that pastors with a liberal drift may not preach on that subject just like happens in liberal churches in the US. However I have never come across such churches).

3. It is not true that the government tells pastors what they can or cannot preach.

4. It is not true that pastors of registered churches receive their salaries from the government and thus have to be subservient to the government.

5. It is true, however, that in some areas the government makes land available free of charge to registered churches so that they can construct church buildings. Also, in the early 80s when churches were struggling to get newly established, it may have happened that in some cases assistance was given by the government.

6. It is not true that manuscripts of sermons have to be submitted to the government before delivery.

7. It is not true that Religious Affairs Bureau (RAB) officials indoctrinate seminary students with communistic ideologies while giving lectures on sociological subjects in seminaries (such as legal rights of Christians and their responsibilities as pastors to the community).

8. It is not true that a list of newly baptized members has to be submitted to the government as it was sometimes done before the Cultural Revolution.

9. It is true, however, that registered churches give annual reports related to finances, number of baptisms, plans of new church buildings and other activities to the government. (If I am not mistaken, audited financial reports have also to be given to government departments in the US).

10. It is not true that "the Chinese government continues to control the financial, leadership, and doctrinal decisions of all registered religious groups…" as reported by the *US Commission on Intl Religious Freedom.* (See rebuttal)

11. It is not true that children under the age of 18 are not permitted to attend church services. Many churches now have Sunday Schools for children

12. It is true what Palau stated: "you don't get arrested unless you break the law."

Rebuttal by China Christian Council
Overseas Relations Department in Shanghai, China
A Letter to "United States Commission on
International Religious Freedom"

Last August, CCC/TSPM (China Christian Council/Three-Self-Patriotic Movement) received a delegation form United States Commission on International Religious Freedom and gave the delegation an introduction of the actual situation of the Protestant churches in China.

After returning to USA, you released the "Policy Focus on China" in which you didn't reflect many truths that you had witnessed by your own eyes in China, and that are worth the gratitude to God from both you and our side. Instead, your description of the religious situation in China is far from being objective, which surprises us awfully. The key tone of that report is "the space for political openness, public activism, and greater civil and individual freedoms is narrowing in China"[1], "the government of China has engaged in systematic and egregious violations of freedom of religion", "the Chinese government, as a matter of policy, monitors, controls, and represses the activities of members of all religious communities"[2], etc. We don't know on which bases that those conclusions are drawn. As a matter of fact, we enjoy more and more religious freedom and get powerful support from the Chinese government. In the past 25 year, we have re-opened and newly constructed more than 55,000 churches and meeting points, 18 theological seminaries and Bible schools as well as a large number of lay training centers. We have cultivated more than 8,000 seminary students (among which most are from and back to the countryside), printed and published 36 million (by 2013 over 100 million) volumes of Bible, 10,000 volumes of Hymnals, 7 million devotionals and 2,5 million audio and visual

---

[1] *Policy Focus on China,* P. 14
[2] Ibid, P. 1

products. Meanwhile, the new campus of Nanjing Union Theological Seminary is under construction (and was finished in 2006). Without the active support from the Chinese government or good religious policy as a guarantee, we can't have scored such great achievements. China is a country with vast territory and rapid development. It's true that the ways of handling things are different in various places and the practice of the religious policy is not fully up to expectations in some places. However, we should look at the mainstream of the matter. The general situation in China is of continuous and rapid development and advancement. We, as Christians, feel that the policy of reform and opening-up formulated by Chinese government is becoming lenient and more active, and that there is more space in the society in that for us to participate. In addition, the Chinese government also encourages religious people to play a more active role in social welfare. China is a country with increasing freedom.

In the report, you also wrote that "Chinese leaders having to refrain from teaching involving the second coming of Jesus, divine healing, the practice of fasting, and the virgin birth because these doctrines or practices are considered by the government to be superstitious or contrary to the Chinese Communist Party's social policies."[3] Since early 1980s, this queer view has become quite popular overseas. Yet, as Chinese Christians, we ourselves have never had such experiences, nor had we found any local government put restrictions on pastoral workers about gospel teaching. Many overseas pastors are also invited to preach in churches when they come to visit China and none of them had such experiences, either. In many churches in China, congregations recite Apostle's Creed in every major service. In the *100 Questions and Answers on the Christian Faith* published by China Christian Council wrote, "Jesus Christ was conceived by the Holy Spirit and born of the Virgin Mary"[4], and "Christ will return to

---

[3] Ibid, P. 3

[4] *100 Questions and Answers on Christian Faith*, P. 28

earth, as He Himself promised."[5] Catechumens in China must pass a catechism examination before the baptism and they must understand such catechism like the virgin birth, the second coming of Jesus, etc. We wonder where from that those blames in the report come. Besides, the report mentioned continually that some people in China are accused of counter-revolutionary and, therefore, put into prison, because of their religious faith. Nevertheless, people with common sense are all supposed to know that the word "counter-revolutionary" was expurgated from Chinese Criminal Law as early as 1997.

The report also reiterates that the Chinese Government should abide by the 1st item of article 18 in International Covenant on Civil and Political Rights, i.e. "Everyone shall have the right to freedom of thought, conscience and religion". However, the 3rd item also states, "Freedom to manifest one's religion or beliefs may be subject only to such limitations as are prescribed by law and are necessary to protect public safety, order, health, or morals or the fundamental rights and freedoms of others". We enjoy the freedom of religious faith, yet freedom also includes responsibility and obligation. Freedom should be based on the respect to other people's fundamental rights and reputation which is in line with the laws. It's also stated in Bible, 'do not use your freedom as a pretext for evil.'[6] Some people do harmful things to others in the name of religion. They are punished not because of faith but of violation of laws. Can American citizens be free from punishment simply because of that they have certain religious faith when they violate American laws?

Every country has its own history, culture, social background and present situation. Every independent country has its own sovereignty which should not be encroached. The Regulations on Religious Affairs issued by Chinese government is in accordance with the real situation of our country, which cannot be judged with the criteria of other countries.

---

[5] Ibid, P. 36

[6] 1 Peter 2: 16

We expect United States Commission on International Religious Freedom to give up your prejudice, dance to another tune, abide by the teaching in the Bible, that is "Let your word be 'Yes, Yes' or 'No, No'"[7], and not to make conclusions that are contrary to the truths. Dialogues rather than antagonism are beneficial to Sino-American people's interests. It's our sincere hope that we can enhance mutual understanding; expand communications with friendly churches and people in USA, and to promote the world peace together.

---

[7] Matthews 5:37

CHAPTER 16

Quo Vadis—China

How did China become what she is today? Did religion play a role? Traveling through this gigantic country with 1.3 billion inhabitants, you will find people following a number of major religions, such as Buddhism, Taoism, Islam, Confucianism, Catholicism and Protestantism. For centuries the teachings of Confucius was paramount in the minds of the Chinese. But as of late, Christianity moved to center stage. Two surveys done by the University of Shanghai and China Partner revealed that close to 45 million Protestant Christians now live in China plus several million Catholics. The Director of SARA (State Administration of Religious Affairs) Wang Zuo'an recently stated, that "the number of religious adherents in China is growing rather quickly." Even the central government in Beijing, which is known for being intensely atheistic, has to admit it.

Foreign missionaries to China played a vital role in this development, as they faithfully spread the gospel throughout difficult times. Let me mention just a few.

Robert Morrison (1782-1834), born in Scotland, was the first Protestant missionary and translated the Bible into Chinese. For twenty-seven years he labored in China (Guangzhou and Macau) and died in Guangzhou.

Karl Gützlaff (1803-51), born in Germany (Prussia), helped Morrison translate the Bible in Guangzhou. He founded the Chinese Evangelization Society, which later sent Hudson Taylor to China. Taylor called Gützlaff the grandfather of the China Inland Mission.

Hudson Taylor (1832-1905), born in England, founded the China Inland Mission. At his death in 1905, there were 205 mission stations with 849 missionaries and 125,000 Chinese converts, and 125 reputable schools. He said, "If I had one thousand British Pounds— China should have it! If I had one thousand lives—China should have them. No! Not China, but Christ! Can we do too much for Him? Can we do enough for such a precious Savior?"

Gladys Aylward (1902-70), born in England, served as an assistant to the Chinese government as a "foot inspector," which enforced the new law against foot binding of young girls. In 1936 she became a Chinese citizen. Her ministry was so profound that a movie was made about her life story: "The Inn of the Sixth Happiness."

Eric Lidell (1902-45), born in China of Scottish parents, and an Olympic gold medalist in the 400 meter event (1924), served as a missionary in China for twenty years (1925-45). He died in Weifeng, Shandong province. A movie "Chariots of Fire" tells his story.

Then there are Chinese pastors, who served as missionaries and ambassadors for Christ in their own country. Let me mention just two.

Watchman Nee (1902-72), born in Fuzhou, Fujian province, found Christ as an eighteen-year-old in 1920. He founded the Little Flock movement. His goal was for each town in China to have one church. He was imprisoned in 1952, later released and died at the age of sixty-nine.

Wang Mingdao (1900-91), born in Beijing, was converted to Christ as a fourteen-year-old, started a church "The Christian Tabernacle," was imprisoned 1957-80, during which time he once was shortly released, when he gave in to the demands of the authorities, but then recanted crying, "I am Peter, I am Peter, I denied my Lord" and thus was thrown back into prison. He died as a hero of the cross.

However, to truly and correctly understand the history of the church in China, we have to study general history at large and go back to AD 435, when the Nestorians were gaining ground in the Middle East. One of the disciples of Nestorius became bishop and established a school in Edessa. In 489 AD the Emperor suppressed the school and expelled its members, who then became missionaries all across that region, and spread the gospel far and wide throughout the then-known Asia.

Another driving force were later the Franciscans, who were people or religious orders who followed the teaching of Francis of Assisi (1182-1226). He had been so impressed by a sermon on Matthew 10.9 that he decided to follow a life of total apostolic poverty. Franciscans became famous by following his convictions and teachings.

Ignatius of Loyola (1491-1556), another great individual, was wounded in battle, which caused him to be converted to Christ. He, with some of his friends, vowed to follow Jesus Christ through poverty, chastity and obedience and made a special vow to submit to the Pope. The Society of Jesuits, which he then founded, desired to first evangelize and then educate their followers to pursue a godly life. Matteo Ricci (1552-1610), a Jesuit, made full use of it. He traveled from Macau to Nanjing, Nanchang and then to Beijing, where he was invited as the first Westerner to enter the Forbidden City. The Emperor invited him to be an advisor to the Imperial court of the Wanli Emperor. He established the Cathedral of the Immaculate Conception in Beijing, and was a respected teacher on astronomy at the court.

Protestants finally arrived on September 4, 1807, as Robert Morrison landed in Macau aboard *Tridend* after 113 days at sea. With this a new chapter of missions to China began. As a result, China has more than 40 million Protestant Christians today, far more than Catholic Christians. In the process of this development, also some strange events took place.

For instance the rise of Hong Xie Quan (1814-64), who as a young man had become interested in the Christian faith by reading some tracts missionaries had given him in Guangzhou. In his studies he came to believe that he is the younger brother of Jesus Christ and felt called to purge Confucianism. He crusaded to abolish foot binding and wanted to socialize land and property. Through his preaching he amassed a huge following, numbering tens of thousands of warriors. Authorities were alarmed to see such a rise in power and tried to eliminate him. He established the "Taiping Heavenly Kingdom" (also called the Heavenly Kingdom of Great Peace) and battled his way into Nanjing, which he then declared the capital of his administration and renamed it Tianjing (Heavenly Capital). The Taiping Rebellion (1850-64) did not achieve its major goal to overthrow the Manchus with their corrupt Qing dynasty, but it caused a colossal loss of lives. Estimate reach from 20 to 30 million! Never before have so many lives been lost in such a short time. It was only equaled a century later under the reign of Mao Zedong, when an estimated 70 million perished (see *The Unknown Story Mao*, page 3). However, after a rather short rule, Hong was overpowered by his enemies and committed suicide.

The Boxer Uprising (1899-1901) was another threat to the followers of the Christian faith. It was enacted by those Chinese, who were anti-foreign and especially anti-missionary. In Beijing alone, two-hundred-thirty foreigners—a number of them diplomats—were murdered. In other parts of China, over two-hundred missionaries with their children and over 30.000 Chinese converts were killed. It was a massacre of historic dimension.

Only one more time since then, and that during Mao Zedong's regime, Christians were under siege. But now China is open for the gospel, and some estimate that half a million people are added to the Church each year.

But the devil is not passive. He never will give up his intrigues and schemes. He is trying other ways to disrupt the advance of the gospel. These are real challenges to China's church. "To conquer is to divide," someone said.

Churches in China now face an assault of liberal theology. During the period of persecution, Christians rallied around the cross. An utter faith in Christ helped them to overcome adversaries. Even during the time when all Bibles were banned, Christians met in homes to encourage each other. Bibles were being hand copied. Christians prayed and believed better times would come. And they did.

But now Christian beliefs are under attack again. In some of the registered churches liberal theology is making a comeback. But also in some of the unregistered house churches false doctrines are being taught. Groups like The Shouters, The Anointed King, Teaching of the Eastern Lightning, The Father Spirit—Mother Spirit Church, The Teaching of the Female Christ and other such groups are rampant all across the country.

Another misconception needs to be cleared up. While Christians were persecuted for their faith during the Cultural Revolution, they now can assemble freely. Churches have sprung up by the thousands all across the land. *Persecution*, in an enormity known then, is no longer the order of the day.

But *prosecution* does take place. The atheistic Chinese government has come forth with rules and regulations that all citizens, including Christians have to abide by. For instance, they can only assemble in government approved church buildings. They cannot hold street meetings. They cannot pass out tracts on streets. And there may be other such restrictions, however, they can live out their faith by following Christ and by living by the teachings of Christ. But they will be prosecuted if they go against the dictates laid down.

Let me give an example what I mean by using another country. Once visiting Yugoslavia during the cold war, when that country was under Soviet domination, I had a unique experience. I had been invited by the Baptist Church to hold evangelistic meetings in their country. True to my principle to abide by the rules, regulations and laws of the land, I was welcomed and could preach in the existing churches all across the land. However, one morning my host, the president of the Baptist Union Dr. Josip Horak, met me with a face displaying great anxiety. "I was told that some members of one of our churches were imprisoned," he said.

"Why," I asked, knowing that this was very uncommon at the time, because Christians in Yugoslavia had learned how to live and behave in a communistic state and therefore were not harassed.

"Listen," he answered, "a group of well-meaning, but amateurish and naïve German Christians had entered our country, and without government approval had left religious tracts in public places. This is forbidden by law. As a consequence, authorities have imprisoned not them—they had disappeared back in their country—but innocent local believers, accusing them to be responsible for acts done by visitors from another country."

I was stunned. But this a good example explaining the difference between *persecution* and *prosecution*. Christians in Yugoslavia were not *persecuted* because of their faith. They were *prosecuted* for doing unlawful things. In this particular case, the local Christians suffered, because the authorities had held them responsible for what had happened. Initially the authorities were not aware that foreigners had deposited those tracts. So they bore the brunt of this.

You often hear people talk about closed doors. Some say that countries are closed to the gospel of Christ. But nowhere in the Bible do we find that countries are closed to the gospel. To the contrary, Christians are exhorted to go! We are to go to the ends of the world!

Actually, closed doors are actually open. Some thought that the former Soviet Union was closed, and then people were surprised when Mikhail Gorbachev (1931-) showed the world his true intention to propagate peace. In 1989 he even was awarded the Nobel Peace Prize. He was the instigator of bringing freedom to his own country and then to all of the Eastern European countries. Thereby the so-called closed doors were revealed to be nothing but a farce. The same can be said about Asia, including China. All of those countries are receptive to the gospel. To God there are no closed doors.

As Christians we must have a distinctive perspective of closed doors. Let us explore three different truths.

1. "Closed doors" have always been open.

Let's see what Paul wrote to the Corinthians: "But I will stay in Ephesus until Pentecost, because a great door for effective work has opened to me, and there are many who oppose me." (1. Cor. 16.8-9). Notice here that Paul does not talk about closed or open doors. He mentions a great door. He wants to encourage us—as he encouraged the Corinthians—to see that we have great and many opportunities for service, even though there might be opposition from adversaries. My father did not see many converts during his missionary career in China, and he could have blamed this as a result to closed doors. He did not. He was simply a pioneer, knowing that God would eventually honor his labor. And I, as his son, have now the privilege to see multitudes of Christians all across China. They are there because others pioneered and persevered. Over 45 million of them!

Paul here also talks about effective work. The German version "reiches Wirken" means rich or bountiful work. What a testimony for Paul to be thrilled in activities that are difficult, yet indispensable and crucial. Paul banked on the Holy Spirit, who will do an effective work amidst adversaries or hindrances. Therefore, we should never be discouraged. With God, all things are possible.

2. "Closed doors" are only those of closed hearts

Just think of Mao's takeover in China! He tried to eradicate all religions, and churches were not allowed to function openly. Persecution took place in a major way. Theological seminaries were shut down, and Bibles and Christian literature were destroyed. Mao tried to stamp out religion, but in finality, he was unsuccessful. In fact, God used him. How? Mao in his desire to eradicate Christianity deported and banished pastors all over the country. With that, however, pastors were able to spread the good news where they were sent. In all those places, churches sprung up and more Chinese were able to hear the gospel. What was meant to be a disaster to the Church of Jesus Christ turned into a blessing—and a great one at that! Hindrances were present, but this did not mean that doors were closed.

The only closed doors are closed hearts. The free will God has given to man enables anyone to make choices. Multitudes of people made the choice to reject God's offer of salvation. Those are closed hearts. And sadly, most prefer to keep their hearts closed.

Scriptures has many examples of closed hearts. When Paul preached to Greek philosophers, they responded, "We want to hear you again on this subject (Acts 17.32). Hear, yes, but not now!

Or take the rich young ruler, whom Jesus met and who had said, that he is following all of the commandments of God. But when Jesus encouraged him to sell everything he had and give it to the poor, he failed. To follow Him was too much for him. So "he went away sorrowful" (Matthew 19.22).

What did the scribes and Pharisees do, when they had a long and extended encounter with Jesus in the temple? When the Jews heard Jesus say, "I tell you the truth, before Abraham was born, I am" they "took up stones to cast Him out" (John 8.59).

Those that have closed hearts are really the ones who are the "closed doors". Countries do not have doors!

Even in tough or impossible situations, God is still in control. What you need is faith, and faith leads to action and action needs perseverance. Above I had mentioned Gladys Aylward, who had been rejected by the leadership of the China Inland Mission. The leaders had good reasons for their decision, however, God had something else in mind. Through her perseverance God was able to bring multitudes into His kingdom.

Only through closed hearts will you find closed doors. Those are the real hindrances or enemies of the gospel.

3. Closed doors are there to be opened

A much quoted verse we find in Revelation 3.20. "Here I am! I stand at the door and knock. If anyone hears my voice and opens the door, I will come in and eat with him and he with me." This reminds me of a lecture I gave at the University of Wuhan. At the close I had encouraged the students to get a Bible to find out how to find God. Mrs. Xie, a professor in philosophy took this seriously and found Christ. She told me later, "I bought a Bible and started to read in it like you told me to, and now I believe."

She had opened her heart.

Here I want to make two observations: Firstly, where doors are open to preach the gospel, heart-doors are often closed, and secondly, where doors are said to be "closed", the heart-doors often pry open. Where doors could be open, like in the western world, the heart-doors are often closed. Humanistic philosophies, liberal theology, evangelical indifferences, and affluent lifestyles are the reasons for this.

However, where doors are so-called "closed", like in areas of the world where it is not allowed to preach openly, the heart-doors seem to be wide open. For instance, in the city of Shenyang, in the north-eastern province Liaoning, a church grew from two-hundred-twenty members to twenty-thousand within a short time. In the year I preached at the church, they had baptized some nine-hundred believers!

Based upon the past, what will the future bring? Some even ask: *What is happening in China today?* But the real question should be: *What will China be like in the future?*

We know that God is doing a mighty work in China today. Some 57.000 church buildings are in operation. The Hallelujah Church in Harbin (Heilongjiang province) has 12.000 members and its Senior

Pastor Lu Dechi recently said, "The Church is playing a more and more important role in China's society." And the senior pastor Rev. Gu of the Chong-Yi Church in Hangzhou has added 8.000 new members within six years. And amazingly, a Communist mayor attends the Zixi Church in the province of Jiangxi! She became a committed Christian while managing her city. We can go on and on relating such stories.

But also on other fronts the church is making tremendous advances. The Amity Bible Printing Press first opened its door in 1987. Since then it has become the largest Bible Printing Establishment in the world. On November 8, 2012 the press celebrated the production of the 100 millionth Bible. Advance printing capacity is 12 million per year. The late Bishop Ting remarked before his death that their aim is to print 1.3 billion Bibles, so that every Chinese will have a Bible.

On my second trip to China in the fall of 1981, I met the former cook of my parents again, whom I then, as a sixteen-old, had not seen since the Ningdu, Jiangxi days. While I had an easy life with wonderful experiences in different parts of the world, he had lived a life of horror, rejection and abandonment. Yet, he had not relinquished his faith, but with other believers in small underground encounters they prayed and had Bible studies. "How that!" I blurted out, "you did not have a Bible nor have you had Bible school training!" "Yes," he said, "but I did remember the Bible stories your parents taught me when I was a teenager."

How marvelous to have heard the story of another one who survived the awfulness of a godless government!

No wonder I had to write the book *Jesus Never Left China*! Also, during that visit the organization China Partner was born in my mind.

It is not only important but also essential for foreigners to partner with the Chinese church. It should be done with the registered and unregistered churches. All of them needed some help, especially during the initial stages of China's opening to the rest of the world. Once I saw the need of a musical instrument in one of the Shanghai churches, so I raised the funds for an organ. Furthermore, when we heard the "Macedonian call" from a house church leader in Wenzhou, we stepped in.

Many have asked whether foreign missionaries should still enter China. Are there responsibilities of the western church towards China? As long as the Three Self Principles are put to use, then the sky is the limit. On the other hand, China's church also has a responsibility to the rest of the world. We in the West can learn from them.

I shall never forget what Bishop Wang had shared with me. He pointed out the enormous suffering Chinese Christians had to go through during the Cultural Revolution (1966-76) and how they succeeded. They came through loud and strong. Wang called it the *Sacrament of Suffering.* And it can only be done with committed prayer. Hudson Taylor once said, "Prayer was never meant to be incidental in the work of God. It is work."

The Ministry of China Partner

China Partner was founded in 1989 to help meet the spiritual needs in China.

China Partner conducts evangelism, pastoral training, and lay leadership courses in major cities across China.

China Partner sends short-term teaching teams to China conducting Pastoral Training Seminars (PTS) in seminaries, Bible schools, and Bible training centers.

China Partner gives free workbooks and notes to pastors and lay leaders in China.

China Partner provides pastors and theological schools mini-libraries at no charge, including reference Bibles, concordances, Bible handbooks and dictionaries, commentaries, etc.

China Partner uploads to the internet training sessions focusing on the following seminars: evangelism, discipleship, Christian leadership, and pastoral care, covering such lessons as "Communicating the Evangelistic Message—Presentation," "Maintaining Spiritual Freshness Through a Devotional Life of Prayer and Study," "Principles of Discipleship," "Mark of a Disciple," "Practical Wisdom for Pastoral Leadership," and lessons on various pastoral issues.

China Partner ministers to Chinese scholars who are studying in North America with the ultimate goal of reaching them with the gospel of Jesus Christ and discipling them. When they return to China, they are potential Christian leaders and influencers of China's future.

China Partner supports Bible school students and grassroots pastors in poverty-stricken parts of China.

China Partner assists in the construction of new churches and Bible school campuses in China.

China Partner builds bridges of friendship, understanding, and communication with the church in China.

China Partner conducts China Symposiums and China Insight Seminars to educate and inform Christians in the West regarding the current church situation in China. The goal is to encourage Christians to pray more effectively for China and to help them participate with their Chinese brothers and sisters in the efforts to reach China with the gospel.

Our Vision: We envision Chinese with the love for Christ, an understanding of the power of God's Word so they can spread the gospel throughout China and the world.

Our Mission: To serve the church in China as they fulfill the Great Commission.

China Partner, Inc.
mail@chinapartner.org
www.chinapartner.org

* * * * *

China Partner has contacts in these nations:
Canada, canada@chinapartner.org
Germany, germany@chinapartner.org
Hong Kong, hongkong@chinapartner.org
New Zealand, newzealand@chinapartner.org
Switzerland, switzerland@chinapartner.org
United States, info@chinapartner.org

Appendix 1

The relevancy of Jesus in our world

Many prominent and legendary names are floating around; however, which name is used more than any other around the globe? What do you know about Alexander the Great, Caesar, Napoleon, Washington, Confucius, Mao or Churchill?

Which name is being used more than any other? Not the ones quoted above. It is Jesus. But what does Jesus mean to you, to me, to all of us? Is He relevant today? How does Jesus influence or affect our world, especially as related to what Jesus expects us to do?

Who remembers the SARS epidemic in China in 2003? Schools and universities in China were closed. Church meetings were cancelled. Whole trains were sprayed and decontaminated. It was a scary time, and many of us were unsure of the future.

And how do you feel in your spirit today? What about another earthquake? Or another epidemic? Or another catastrophe? Are you scared? Am I scared? Do we dream of it? Do we prepare? Or do we just live on. What are our needs?

How does Jesus meet our needs—your and my needs?

The question I asked at the beginning was, "Is Jesus relevant today, and if so, how?" How can *we* handle our sufferings, burdens, needs and fears? How can we live successfully as difficulties, struggles, and adversities stare at us each day? Does Jesus really care about our personal concerns and complexities?

Furthermore, does Jesus really care about those who have never heard about Him?

But let us first talk about our personal needs that affect us in our lives today. For instance, does He care about my severe illness? Some of us suffer from dangerous physical ailments. I had my share of it.

When I was thirty-nine years old and a father of four young children, my doctor informed me after an exam that he would have to perform surgery right away. I was shocked. Could it be cancer? The doctor hesitated before answering my anxious question, "Will radiation be necessary after surgery?" "It is possible," he finally said. Then I knew. It was cancer!

The next afternoon I was resting on our bed and our only little girl, just three years old, (we have three boys older than her) was taking her nap beside me. Little girls look like angels when they sleep. They are so innocent. They are so lovable. All of a sudden a horrible thought hit me. Maybe I will never see her grow up, and maybe I will never be able to lead her down the aisle as a young bride to meet her groom.

A battle was raging in my soul. Tears filled my eyes. My wife came in at that moment and asked, "What is it darling, why are you crying?" I told her my thoughts, and then added, "This battle I have to fight alone, honey. Nobody can help me now, not you, nor my parents, no friend or pastor, but only the Lord himself."

The peace I had known before was gone.

That evening I went out alone into the fields surrounding our village near Frankfurt, Germany, where we lived at the time, and I wrestled with God. I battled it out with MY GOD. I was still young and did not want to die and leave my family and ministry. After all, I was only thirty-nine years old! A whole life with interesting and exciting events remained stretched out before me. And now cancer?

In those days there were not many options to cure the kind of cancer I had. I fought that inner and intense battle raging within me for a long time, a battle I had never fought before. My mind went whirling around. The inner peace I had known since my conversion as a teenager was gone. The inner turmoil and confusion was overwhelming.

Finally, I threw myself prostrate on the dusty path and pleaded with God. One thing I knew: He wanted to teach me something. He wanted to teach me total trust and a complete dedication and an ultimate acceptance of His divine will! I had to come to the point of acknowledging what He had in store for me, no matter what.

As I was laying on that dusty path, I was at last able to pray, "My life is in your hands, do with me what you want. It's alright whether I live or die. But now I need peace of heart. Please give me back the peace I had known for so many years."

The miracle happened. God came through. Suddenly the peace of God came down with crucial force flooding my entire being in a powerful way. God had met me there on that solitary path. I got up and went home rejoicing in my God and my Savior.

Where are you today? What are your concerns?

Are you afraid? Are you unsure of the future? Have you lost your job? Are you ill? Have you lost the peace in your heart? Do you need a new encounter with your God?

So who is Jesus? What does He mean to you, to me—to all of us? Can I put my trust in Him? Really? Can I leave my burdens with him? Does He know and care about my difficulties? Does He really care about me and can He take my fears away?

But then we need to go beyond our personal needs and look at the needs of the world! There are great needs! For one, millions of people have never heard about Jesus and who He really is. That is why we are involved in world missions!

Let us once more look into the Scriptures. (Mark 5. 1-13. 18-20). I want to zero in on four areas:

1. There is no place where Jesus does not go

2. There is no power that Jesus cannot conquer

3. There is no person who Jesus cannot save

4. There is no person who Jesus has saved whom He cannot use

1. There is no place where Jesus does not go (vs. 2)

Jesus came into the region of the Gadarenes at the Sea of Galilee. Jesus cares about all people. When he was on earth he went from place to place. He loved all the people and wanted to reach out to them.

Here he encountered a man with an evil spirit. He was in great need. He lived in a cemetery among tombs. No one could tame him and finally he was abandoned. But Jesus was ready to meet him. Jesus actually did not have to go there. There were nicer places than the tombs in a cemetery. But Jesus knew exactly what he wanted and needed to do. He wanted to help people in need. And here was one in terrible need.

After three years of amazing ministry and before Jesus left this earth He told his disciples: "Go into all the world and preach the Gospel to all creation." This command is still valid today. It was never cancelled. A command has to be cancelled to nullify it. So the command stands.

How does Jesus come to all people in the world today? Jesus comes today in the person of his disciples, his followers. No place is too far or too near. My parents ministered for twenty-five years in the country where I was born and where I grew up. I have worked alongside my Chinese brothers and sisters for the last thirty years. Today our eldest son Erik has taken over the ministry as president. Why do we go? Because there are multitudes of people in China that need to know about the love of Jesus and his forgiveness. People everywhere need to hear about Jesus.

In Cairo, Egypt, I once visited the so called "garbage city", where people with their families literally live on garbage dumps. The poorest of the poor call this home and eke out a meager living by scouring the city during the night for garbage, taking what they find to the garbage city and then sifting through and salvaging anything that still can be sold or used.

For many years no one had cared about the people of that garbage city. Not even Christians. Then a Presbyterian pastor living in Cairo heard about these people and began to visit them. Men and women came to know the love of Christ, and today there is a vibrant church— right on the garbage dump! Jesus would also have gone there.

And as Jesus goes to China and to the garbage city in Cairo, so he comes to you. He comes to you personally.

But you say: "I have different problems than the evangelization of the world. I am very ill and need healing. I am in deep financial trouble and need help to pay my debts. I have a kid that is into drugs. My husband left me. I lost my job, and don't know how to make ends meet.

Jesus is here to help you. He knows about your needs and problems. However, you have to surrender to Him. Are you ready to give your life over totally to Him? Are you ready to throw your burdens on him? Only when you are willing to do so, will the peace of God fill your heart. <u>There is no place where Jesus does not go</u>! He comes also to you! But more, Jesus now needs you to go beyond your needs.

2.   There is no power that Jesus cannot conquer (vs. 3-5)

In our story we read of a man who was possessed by an evil spirit. Nobody was able to help him. But Jesus came.

But there are many evil spirits or powers that bind us. The power of terror, the power of worry, the power of fear when natural disaster strikes.

Natural disasters are mysteries to us. The Tsunami in Asia, hurricane Katrina in New Orleans, the earthquake in Sichuan or the bushfires in Australia, and the flooding in Bangladesh.

However, as Christians we know that nothing happens without the will of God. He is in control–always. All powers and every terror Jesus can handle. He is able to conquer everything.

So often we have a hard time accepting our burdens. Yes, it was terribly difficult for me to accept my serious bout with cancer. Only after surrendering completely to the will of God was I able to have victory. God could have dealt with me in a different way. When I was lying in that hospital bed, a man from our church was also battling cancer. He was on the floor above me. The Elders came and anointed him with oil and prayed over him just like they had done for me. But he died. Why did he have to die and why was I allowed to live? This will always be a mystery to me. There are often situations in life that we cannot explain, but also in those situations we must be willing to surrender to God's perfect will and remember that God is good and he is in control.

<u>There is no power that Jesus cannot conquer.</u>

3.   There is no person whom Jesus cannot save (vs. 3)

In this story there was a man who was completely lost and helpless. Nobody could help him. But Jesus helps those who cannot be helped and who cannot help themselves.

The greatest need is the spiritual need. All over the world, people are searching for peace of mind and peace of heart. Why? Because something is missing in their lives. Where do I come from? Why am I here? Where am I going when I die? These are profound questions that need to be answered.

Also, many cannot cope with their sins.

In Boca Raton where I live, I met a Chinese student studying at

Florida Atlantic University. His name is Ming Ming. He had never heard of Jesus. His parents are atheists, and he was raised in an atheistic society. My wife and I befriended him for months. He came to our church. Then in a restaurant I explained the gospel to him and right there and then, he accepted Christ. Who would have believed that this young atheist with a background like his would come to faith in Christ?

<u>There is no man that Jesus cannot save.</u>

4. There is no person once saved whom He cannot use (vs. 18-20)

The once tormented man became a missionary. Just imagine! The one whom no one could tame becomes a missionary!

Since his conversion to Christ we have followed up with Ming Ming. He had many questions. "Where did Abel get his wife? Who created God? Why do we have so many wars?" Ming Ming is still a very young Christian. Several months after his conversion to Christ he went with a College group from our church to New Orleans on a missions trip. He wants to serve Christ. He is a happy believing Christian now. His life has purpose and meaning. He witnesses to his Chinese friends about his faith. When he visited his parents in Changsha, he witnessed to them. He desires for them to find his Savior. Later he led his roommate Alex to Christ. Then he married his high school sweetheart and she accepted Christ. Alex brought his wife Jingnan over to Boca and a few weeks ago, she came to Christ. Now there are four Chinese students, two of them PhD students, who now are believers.

<u>There is no person who Jesus has saved whom He cannot use</u>
Jesus wants to use all of us!

What are our problems today? Do we fight temptations? Do we try to cope with the pain of losing a loved one? Do we fight against a terrible disease? Are we afraid of the future? Are we scared of another earthquake or typhoon?

Are we worriers, worrying about every aspect of our lives, or are we warriors—warriors of the Cross?

Do you know what gives me hope? It is the cross of Christ. The center of the Christian faith is the cross of Jesus. Even throughout China now thousands of red crosses are visible on churches everywhere, the symbol of Christianity. In each Christian church across the world, you find the symbol of a cross. Only through the cross we find peace; peace in our fears and anxieties; peace in our cares and burdens and in the throes of death; peace in our ailments and peace when politicians disappoint us.

But there is more than that. As Christians each of us has been called to serve our Lord in some way, each in our own sphere of influence: In school, in our jobs, in offices, sports arenas, shops, neighborhoods and yes, on the mission fields of the world.

Are you involved in missions? What are you doing to reach the lost for Christ? What are you doing to reach people across this world?

Remember:

- There is no place where Jesus does not go
- There is no power that Jesus cannot conquer
- There is no person whom Jesus cannot save
- There is no person who Jesus has saved whom He cannot use

Is Jesus relevant today? Yes, and yes again. Does he have a mission for you and for me? Yes, and yes again.

Therefore, go in peace and find out what *your* mission is. And then go and reach out to the world.

Appendix 2

Provisions on the Administration of Religious Activities of Aliens within the Territory of the People's Republic of China

**Decree No. 144 of The State Council Signed By
Premier Li Peng On January 31, 1994**

Article 1. These provisions are formulated in accordance with the Constitution in order to ensure the freedom of religious belief of aliens within the territory of the People's Republic of China and to maintain the public interests of the society.

Article 2. The People's Republic of China respects the freedom of religious belief of aliens within Chinese territory and protects friendly contacts and cultural and academic exchanges of aliens with Chinese religious circles in respect of religion.

Article 3. Aliens may participate in religious activities at Buddhist monasteries, Taoist temples, mosques, churches, and other sites for religious activities within Chinese territory. Aliens may preach and expound the scripture at Chinese sites for religious activities at the invitation of Chinese religious bodies at or above the level of provinces, autonomous regions, and municipalities directly under the Central Government206 • Jesus Never Left China

Article 4. Aliens may hold religious activities attended by aliens at the sites for religious activities approved by the department of religious affairs of the people's government at or above the county level.

Article 5. Aliens within Chinese territory may invite Chinese religious personnel to conduct such religious ceremonies as baptism, weddings, funerals, and Taoist and Buddhist rites.

Article 6. Aliens entering Chinese territory may carry religious printed matter, religious audio-visual products, and other religious articles for personal use; if the amount of such religious printed matters, religious audio-visual products, and other religious articles is greater than for personal use, it shall be dealt with in accordance with the provisions of the Chinese Customs.

Religious printed matter or religious audio-visual products whose contents are detrimental to the public interests of Chinese society are forbidden to bring into Chinese territory.

Article 7. Aliens within Chinese territory shall recruit the persons to study abroad to be trained as religious personnel, or come to study or teach at Chinese religious institutions in accordance with the relevant provisions of China.

Article 8. Aliens who conduct religious activities within Chinese territory shall abide by Chinese laws and regulations and shall not establish religious organizations, set up religious offices or sites for religious activities, or run religious institutions within Chinese territory, nor may they develop followers, appoint religious personnel, or engage in other missionary activities.

Article 9. Where aliens conduct religious activities that violate these Provisions, the department of religious affairs and other related departments of the people's government at or above the county level shall dissuade or stop them; where those activities violate the control of the entry and exit of aliens or administration of public security, the public security organs shall punish them in accordance with the law; where a crime is constituted, they shall be investigated for their criminal responsibility by the judicial organs.

Appendix 1: Provisions on the Administration of
Religious Activities of Aliens within the Territory
of the People's Republic of China • 207

Article 10. These Provisions are applicable to religious activities of foreign bodies within Chinese territory.

Article 11. Chinese citizens residing abroad within Chinese territory, Taiwan residents on the Mainland, and the residents of Hong Kong and Macao in the inland, shall conduct religious activities with reference to these Provisions.

Article 12. The department of religious affairs of the State Council shall be responsible for the interpretation of these Provisions.

Article 13. These Provisions shall enter into force as of the day of promulgation.[8]

---

[8] "Regulations on Religious Affairs," ISBN 7-80123-663-7. This booklet is in Chinese and English and was published in China in 2005.• 209 •

About the Author

Werner Bürklin was born in Wuhu, China, in 1930. His parents were German Christian missionaries. He earned is doctoral degree at Luther Rice College & Seminary, Atlanta, Georgia. A longtime evangelist, he founded China Partner, Inc., to equip young leaders for Christian ministry. He and his wife live in Boca Raton, Florida.

Printed in the United States
By Bookmasters